Life is Breath;
Everything Else is a Story

My Story, Your Story, Our Story, The Story

by Pamela Harman Daugavietis

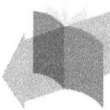

Chapbook Press

Schuler Books
2660 28th Street SE
Grand Rapids, MI 49512
(616) 942-7330
www.schulerbooks.com

Life is Breath; Everything Else Is a Story

ISBN 13: 9781957169309

Library of Congress Control Number: 2023900386

Printed in the United States by Chapbook Press.

The breath is a form of prayer, the life-force itself,
the holy spirit that binds us to the mind of God.
—Joan Borysenko

Those who tell the stories rule society.
—Plato

Dedication

Shortly after Andy and I moved to Grand Rapids in 1991, I met Bill Martindill, a Board member at Butterworth Hospital. Bill was in his early 80s and I would soon turn 50. Bill reminded me of my father—a devoted husband, family man, self-made businessman and community volunteer. Both were born in 1910, but my dad died at age 77 of Alzheimer's disease; Bill, who always said, "Growing older is inevitable; growing old is optional," lived to be 100. Like my dad, Bill was a great storyteller. Both of them encouraged me to keep writing, reading, and sharing my own life stories. Bill said the best way for "us elders" to pass on our hard-earned, life-affirming lessons is through stories, " . . . so the next generation can get smart sooner than we did." My dad, in a handwritten letter to me on October 7, 1970, said, "Write about what you love. Don't worry about getting it published or as a way to make some money. You have natural talent you want and need to share. The rest will take care of itself." My mother, as you will read in a few of the stories to follow, was and continues to be my Rock of Gibraltar. Both she and my Aunt Charlotte, my dad's younger sister, taught me the value of family history. Thus, this book is lovingly dedicated to Edwin Webb and Mary Ellen Moore Harman, Charlotte Harman Harvey Littlefield, and William "Bill" Martindill.

Thank you!

To Pierre Camy for his encouragement and support in helping me self-publish this collection of stories at Schuler Books & Music in Grand Rapids, MI; and to Wikipedia and other reliable on-line sources of credible facts and resources; to our Cascade Library and public libraries everywhere for the numerous resources they provide free-of-charge to inform, enlighten and inspire those of all ages and life circumstances; to my parents and grandparents who told me stories growing up that taught me lasting and valuable life lessons; to family and friends who've encouraged me to keep writing, many of whom are mentioned in the stories that follow; to those special friends and colleagues who agreed to read my first draft and gave suggestions for improvement; and to my dear husband Andy, my greatest supporter, cheerleader, confidant, and trustworthy life partner, the first to read the following book cover to cover and with a few valuable suggestions to make it better, gave it a high-five.

Table of Contents

Prologue

We live our lives forward but we understand them backwards.
—Søren Kierkegaard

In the spring of 2021, I signed up for an online course on conscious aging with the Institute of Noetic Sciences[1]. Near the end of one of the sessions, we 'seniors,' men and women ages 70 to 90 from countries around the world, listened to each other share stories about how COVID-19 had altered our lives and how we were coping, or not. We were then given a journaling prompt and 10 minutes to write whatever came to mind.

This is what I wrote:

"What's my next priority? Is it to simplify my life and continue downsizing the belongings my husband and I have accumulated over the years? Or is it to finally gather together stories I've written since the lockdown began about what it's like to grow older while living through a pandemic, a new experience for all of us, regardless of age and life circumstances.

"Sadly our world today feels so chaotic and divisive. Our United States of America can be more accurately described as the divided states of America. Perhaps what we elders are being called upon to do now is write stories about what we've learned in the past, who we are today and why, what gives our lives purpose and meaning and our goals and dreams for the future. We need stories of distilled wisdom to remind us of our worth and debunk society's false assumption of our irrelevance as we grow older. We need stories about being grateful to be alive at such a pivotal time, stories that bring us together rather than tear us apart, stories that make us laugh and cry, and stories we can leave behind to encourage, inspire and enlighten younger ones coming after us."

Later that spring, *The Wall Street Journal* published an article by Peter Funt titled *An Epidemic of Memoir Writing*. In it Mr. Funt said memoir writing had obviously become a fad during the Covid lockdown

---

[1] https://noetic.org/

because everyone is doing it, including non-celebrities whose lives aren't very important or interesting.

I was surprised at Mr. Funt's failure to mention honest memoir writing as a benefit to the one writing it as much or more than it is to the one reading it. Thus, I sent an email to the editor the very next day expressing my views.

A week later, a distilled version of my letter to the editor appeared on page A16 of *The Wall Street Journal*.

In respectful response to Peter Funt's Op-Ed, 'An epidemic of Memoir-Writing': I am a 79-year-old retired freelance writer working on my third memoir after self-publishing two, purchased by a few and, as far as I know, read only by a handful of family members and friends. So why am I writing a third? I love to write. I love to read others' stories when written from the heart, not to impress but to express. Our world would be improved if we spent more time in self-reflection during this time of Covid-19. Pamela Daugavietis, Grand Rapids, Michigan.

Some of the stories that follow were written years ago and edited, and some were written recently. Gathering them together for a book I've been wanting to write since Covid began—both memoir and a "Suggestions-on-How-to-Write-Your-Own-Life-Stories" book—has given me a new perspective on growing older. Now more content with 'what is' and where I am, I see my life today as a rich tapestry of joys and sorrows, changes and challenges, gains and losses, good days and not-so-good days, with even the not-so-good days bringing joy and new insights and wisdom.

After listening to the stories of so many others from here at home and around the world, I've come to realize that my story and your story are as much the same as they are different; and that our story as human beings with differences in race, gender, religion, culture, intellect, intelligence, or somewhere in between, are the same as they are different, which is why I decided to write *Life is Breath, Everything Else is a Story*.

Hopefully, by reading a few stories that follow of memorable "teaching moments" and a few turning points in my life will inspire and encourage you, dear reader, to begin writing stories from your own life.

We who are alive today are living through a time of great change. Sun Tzu, Chinese military general, strategist, philosopher, and writer (544-496 B.C.) said, "In the midst of chaos, there is also opportunity." Many sages from past times have also declared that chaos brings new creativity and awareness, a higher consciousness about what it means to be human, to be alive, whether we are young, middle-age or older.

So check out the variety of resources in the appendix that have been helpful to me with the hope that they will be helpful to you, as well. And if, like me, you enjoy writing, reading and sharing stories, I encourage you to write on, write on, write on!

Chapter 1: In the Middle All The Way
God loves you more.
—Reverend Harold Buckley

So how did a nice, white girl born in the middle of May, in the middle of World War II, in the middle of Ohio, the middle daughter of a middle-class family, in the Methodist Church, later become how I describe myself today as an ecumenical Christian from a Buddhist perspective? Looking back on my life, I realize my faith in God and my lifelong desire to be a follower of Jesus, were first handed down to me through stories my mother and aunt preserved and shared with me of generations of my forefathers and mothers from England, Ireland and Scotland, who survived far worst challenges than I ever have.

While the story about how I learned about Buddhism is in Chapter 18 that follows, the story about when I first learned the importance and power of faith goes back to Mother's Day in 1953, two days before my tenth birthday. My parents, two sisters and I were sitting in our regular pew at the Worthington Methodist Church as Reverend Buckley began his sermon about mothers. He described how his own mother had cared for him and his siblings during the Great Depression with kindness, courage, and sacrifice to herself so her children wouldn't go hungry or be afraid of what the future might bring. He said she never lost faith that somehow God would provide for them all, and He did.

Reverend Buckley then went on to say his mother taught him virtues and values she learned from her own parents. Although she died some years earlier, he still felt her loving presence and guidance with him every day.

Reverend Buckley looked up, paused, then glanced across the room to where we were sitting. I felt as if he was looking directly at me when he said, "While mother love is the greatest of human loves, God loves you more."

Those were the days I imagined God as a bearded old white man sitting on a throne deciding at the time of our death whether we deserve to go to heaven, or 'you know where'. And while I can't say Reverend

Buckley's words entirely shifted my thinking about God in that moment, they aroused my curiosity about who God was. It was then I started thinking about God as someone or something beyond a fearsome and judgmental old man.

Today, as I look back on my life and all that I've experienced, the good, bad and everything in between, I know I've been held up, guided, consoled and cared for by God's grace every step of the way. I now perceive God as the unnameable and pure presence—the Lasting, Omnipresent, Vital Energy—that created and sustains our universe and life itself through love.

Even at a young age, I wondered why in church we were taught to love and forgive our enemies but once church was over and we got back to our everyday lives in the "real world," we acted differently. As Father Richard Rohr says in his book, *Essential Teachings on Love*[2], "Jesus did not say, 'Worship me,' but he often said, 'Follow me.'" To me, Jesus taught us to first love God who gave us the gift of life and that it's good to be human, and that our gift back to God is to love ourselves as God loves us so we can love others better. Many call this The Circle of Life.

What I've also realized in my later years is that the greatest gift God gave me after the gift of life is the gift of choice—the freedom to choose what I think, say, and do that creates the quality of my day. I've always loved this quote by Wolfgang Mozart (1756–1791), who said, "The music is not in the notes, but in the silence between the notes." While he lived more than 200 years ago, Mozart's wisdom, like his music, is timeless. It's 'the pause-between-cause' or 'trigger' that teaches wisdom. It's my choice in how to respond in all kinds of situations that makes all the difference in my day going forward, which I, in turn, pass on to others in the way I choose to interact with them throughout the day.

To me, the third immutable law of life is change. Stories are narratives about how and why what happens to us day by day changes us, teaches us wisdom, makes us more forgiving of self and others, and gives our lives purpose and meaning, regardless of our age.

---

2 ©2018 Center for Action and Contemplation

Chapter 2 ~ Mother Love

The hand that rocks the cradle rules the world
—William Ross Wallace

For a woman born in 1907, on a small farm in rural Newark, Ohio, to parents as mismatched as any two parents can be, my mother became as accomplished, disciplined, generous, wise and caring as anyone I have ever known. As the oldest of four children, Mother appreciated, loved and forgave her own parents in spite of their inability to be good parents themselves. Yet she never let their unhappiness stop her from achieving her own happiness first as a career woman in the 1930's, then a wife, mother, homemaker and community volunteer.

Thus, it was Mother who taught me a lesson at a critical time in my own life that only she could teach. When my grades at Ohio State went from A's and B's to C's and D's, after my longtime boyfriend I thought would someday be my husband broke up with me, Mother told me she and Daddy wouldn't pay for my tuition unless my grades improved. I knew Mother meant business. The college party scene wasn't for me, and I felt adrift socially, torn between wanting to fit in, yet not wanting to be like others too 'wild' for my tastes. Besides, I was a townie, so I lived at home where I spent a lot of time alone, in my room, writing in my journal and pondering my future.

Thanks to Miss Murray, my fourth grade teacher, Miss Burnside, my high school English teacher, and Mother, who worked at *The Ohio State Journal* for 14 years as assistant to Edgar Wolfe, editor and publisher, I decided to switch my major from Arts and Sciences to Broadcast Journalism. I also applied for and was hired as a part-time editorial clerk at *The Columbus Citizen-Journal* so I could begin saving my own money. Mother became my biggest fan and encourager as I earned A's on stories I wrote for *The Lantern*, OSU's student newspaper, and book reviews for *The Journal*.

Years later, Mother's positive response when I told her Andy and I were engaged, and two weeks later telling her we would be going to Saudi Arabia to live and work for a few years, gave me the confidence I needed to better respond to a barrage of horrified comments others were making about where we were heading after our wedding.

Even into her 80s, Mother's zest for each new day never diminished for whatever she had to do during and after having to sell Daddy's business and care for him for five years before his death in 1987 with Alzheimer's disease.

After Andy and I returned from Saudi Arabia in 1991, and until Mother died in February of 1993, we'd visit her in Worthington, every two or three months. Every time she opened her front door to greet us, I couldn't help but notice how different she looked from the way she sounded on the phone. During our weekly telephone calls, it was easy to forget she was in her 80s. She sounded more like a 40- or 50-year-old— enthusiastic, energetic and full of life. I loved listening to her describe her days as hectic, and grateful too, that she broke the stereotype of the lonesome widow living alone, grieving the past with time on her hands, complaining about aches and pains. She had many caring friends and family members besides her three daughters she regularly stayed in touch with, including her six grandchildren.

To the casual observer, Mother's life, no doubt, seemed perfect, albeit ordinary. A long and happy marriage to a successful and loving husband, three adoring daughters, relatively good health, many friends, a comfortable home— Mother's life was surely blessed, though far from ordinary. Unknown to most of her friends and even some family members, she faced obstacles in her life that required exceptional fortitude, wisdom and personal agency to overcome.

If I had to choose one bit of wise advice Mother left with me when she died, it would be what she often told me when I felt discouraged and disheartened.

"You can't be a best friend to others until you're best friends with yourself, Pammy" she'd say. Mother's sound advice took me years to learn; once I did, I've never forgotten it. Loving ourselves is not selfish. Loving ourselves first enables us to be more authentic with others, and to love others for who they truly are, too.

Chapter 3: We Are Made of Star Stuff
Science is but an image of the truth.
—Francis Bacon

On the first day of winter quarter my freshman year at Ohio State, our professor in General Botany 401, a short, thin, frail looking older woman came to life the minute the bell rang. After briefly welcoming us students, she began walking around the room telling us about her lifelong passion for growing things. We sat spellbound and wide-eyed watching her move about the room, waving her arms and pointing along the wall to posters with images of all kinds of growing things. Listening to her explain the difference between biomass, biosphere and bulbs, and fondling the leaves of growing things on the windowsill piqued my interest in a class I signed up for as a requirement, not because I shared her passion for plants. She spoke of grasses and shrubs, trees and bushes as if they were all conscious beings, never mentioning God or a Divine Creator. Rather, she implied "growing things" have more intelligence than humans.

In the weeks to come, when we'd peer through our microscopes at leaf specimens from various varieties of trees, she'd point out that while the patterns in all of them were different in shape, size, color and texture, all of them had sameness in cell structure and structural configuration, regardless of genus or species. She reiterated they were alike in some ways, different in others, just like us humans.

In my junior year at Ohio State, when I began working night shift at *The Columbus Citizen-Journal*, one of my jobs was to write book reviews and obituaries. Every Monday, the city editor handed out newly published books for us to select, read, and write a brief review for the Friday edition.

One book in particular caught my eye immediately: *View From a Distant Star: Man's Future in the Universe* by Harlow Shapley. I was hooked after reading the first two paragraphs of the book's Preface:

Mankind is made of star stuff, ruled by universal laws. The thread of cosmic evolution runs through his history, as through all phases of the universe—the microcosmos of atomic structures, molecular forms, and microscopic organisms, and the macrocosmos of higher organisms, of plants, stars, and galaxies. Evolution is still proceeding in galaxies and man—to what end, we can only vaguely surmise.

Is man here to stay? Can he survive the rigors of his harsh environment? He has himself made it harsh by adding to the natural hazards greater ones of his own making. Population pressures and the fruits of his science and technology now threaten his future. His lifetime on our small planet will depend on how well he understands the requirements for survival and how willing he is to struggle for the peaceful creation of a viable world society.

Two weeks later, my review of Shapley's book, published in 1963, appeared in the *Citizen-Journal,* my first-ever byline in a big-city newspaper. Sadly, a copy of my review was lost over time, but I recall writing that I had never read anything so poetic yet so realistically descriptive of how our country and the world felt to me during the chaotic 60's, morally upended and seriously precarious, yet the final outcome would be up to us, as Shapley said.

My senior year at Ohio State, I signed up for Descriptive Astronomy 500 taught by a man younger than my botany professor and with the same passion for stars, planets and galaxies, as she had for plants, trees and bushes. Gazing into the night sky through the off-campus telescope north of Columbus, I felt the same awe and wonderment I experienced looking into my microscope in Botany 401, seeing patterns of design and movement in the heavens held together by gravity and centrifugal force reaching throughout the Universe, a concept so immense, yet so personal and comforting. What I realized after taking both classes is that there *is* a divine order to the Universe.

However, the question remains, even 60 years later—why is it taking us, and our national and global leaders so long to come up with a plan we can all agree on, participate in and continue to support in order to assure a sustainable, just, peaceful and prosperous world for all? And while we've made significant progress in this direction, there is still much work to be done. One goal I feel is not only attainable but also doable is for the male and female "energies" in however they're defined and lived, must be in a dynamic, creative and non-dualistic partnership, rather than a power struggle.

Thus, with all humility, I close with my slightly revised version of the second opening paragraph of Shapley's preface, based on what is transpiring around our world today. In the stories that follow, I will continue to attempt to adjust gender references in a similar way to reflect how I feel about humanity coming together in, and with, our diversity as a United human family rather than a Divided human family. We must be who we are, who God created each one of us to be, while continuing to heal the wounds of the past. We can and must evolve into a higher consciousness to learn, to wake up, grow up and work together to preserve and protect life and our beloved and beautiful home on Mother Earth for perpetuity. Diversity is a strength, not a weakness.

> *Is humanity here to stay? Can we survive the rigors of our harsh environment? We ourselves have made it harsh by adding to the natural hazards greater ones of our own making. Population pressures and the fruits of our science and technology now threaten our collective future. Our shared lifetime on our small planet will depend on how well we understand the requirements for survival and how willing we are to struggle for the peaceful creation of a viable world society for all life.*

Chapter 4: Where Did Bobby Come From?

The single most important key to success is to be a good listener.
—Kelly Wearstler

In the early fall of 1972, our adult study group at First Presbyterian Church in Petoskey planned a Sunday afternoon family outing and picnic in a nearby park. Since my husband was out of town, I hired a babysitter to stay home with 5-month-old Bobby so he wouldn't miss his usual afternoon nap. John, 4, and I, went to the park by ourselves.

After socializing and games, I realized I had forgotten my dish to pass. One of the mothers offered to keep an eye on John while I went home to get my macaroni salad. Bobby was up from his nap, so I drove the babysitter home and brought Bobby back with me. We lived only 10 minutes from the park, so John never knew I was away.

When it came time to go home, John climbed into the front seat next to me. I strapped Bobby into his infant seat and put him on the floor of our Volkswagen camper. Just as we were pulling out of the parking lot, John asked a question I wasn't expecting.

"Where did Bobby come from?"

Some of my friends had older children asking questions about what many were still referring to as "the birds and the bees." Parents in the early 70s were beginning to teach their kids "the facts of life" more openly and honestly, something few parents did when I was growing up. I assumed John was ready to know more about something he didn't understand, so I took a deep breath and began.

"Well, John, it's like this. . . . . mommies and daddies who are married and love each other come together in a way that enables Daddy to plant a sperm inside Mommy's body where it grows into a baby nine months later."

I paused, certain my brief explanation was sufficient for now.

"Mom," John said firmly, "you didn't answer my question."

"I didn't?"

"No. When we came today, Bobby wasn't with us.

Now he's in the backseat. Where did Bobby come from?"

What I learned that day and even now occasionally forget is to make sure I understand the question before I expound on extraneous details that don't even begin to answer the question asked.

Whoever wants or needs your opinion or explanation will appreciate your request for clarification before launching into a long winded oration that misses the mark. Besides, you will be spared feeling foolish and being ignored for going on and on about something irrelevant to their inquiry and embarrassing yourself even more.

Chapter 5: Bobby's Ah-ha Moment!

A miracle is a shift in perception.
—Marianne Williamson

John, 6, was in school. Bobby, 3, was playing in the living room while I busied myself in the kitchen. Glancing at the clock, I saw it was nearly time for lunch. I told Bobby to put away his playthings so we could run an errand. Toys, crayons and coloring books were strewn all over the floor. When he balked, I said we couldn't leave until he picked up his toys. Three times I reminded him. He wasn't budging.

The phone rang. It was Mrs. Brown. Next to Bobby's big brother John, Bing Brown was Bobby's best friend in the whole world.

"I have errands to run up your way," Mrs. Brown said. "May I drop Bing off so the boys can play?"

"Bobby and I need to run a quick errand first," I said. "Come in half an hour. The boys can eat lunch together."

When I told Bobby that Bing was coming, he began jumping up and down and clapping his hands.

"Remember," I said, "we have to run to the store first, but not until you clean up your toys."

Bobby's smile vanished as he stuck out his lower lip, crossed his arms, and dropped to his knees in a serious pout.

"We're not leaving until you clean up this room," I said as sympathetically yet as firmly as I could. "The sooner we go, the sooner we'll get back."

I turned toward the kitchen, glancing back a few seconds later to see if Bobby was picking up his toys. Instead, he appeared motionless, sitting on his haunches, hands on his hips, eyes wide open as if a light bulb had just switched on in his head.

"The sooner we go, the sooner we'll get back," he repeated to himself out loud—twice.

No sooner said than done, Bobby swung into action, picking up his crayons, coloring books, toy cars and trucks, picture books, puzzles and blocks and put them all away.

"Ready to go, Mom," he said proudly, standing by the front door. The living room never looked tidier. Both of us were smiling.

Years later, I discovered *A Course in Miracles*, by Helen Schucman, former professor of medical psychology at Columbia University, who describes a miracle as a shift in perception. Reading this caused me to recall Bobby's "miracle" that occurred so long ago thanks to his own "shift in perception." Even as a three-year-old he solved his own dilemma thereby shifting the atmosphere of his day, and my day, as well.

Obviously, cause and effect is a foundational truth best learned early in life. When someone interferes with this immutable law, many times with good intentions by wanting to help or gain favor, we never learn the timelessness of this simple equation and the need for every individual to learn for themselves.

Thoughts create desire, desire creates energy, energy and choice create action, and action fulfills desire. It's a flow of energy I can see in my own life when I was sustained and motivated by faith not to give up when I faced unexpected losses and challenges. Bobby took responsibility (the ability to respond) once he became motivated by desire and understood that *he* controlled the outcome (playing with Bing), but only until *he himself* made it happen. He understood he was in charge and acted on it!

I'm not saying this one incident in Bobby's childhood was responsible for shaping the direction of his adult life. Yet, it illustrates a pattern I am grateful he and his brother John learned well by the time they became adults. Thoughts become things. Change your thinking, change your life. We create our own reality by our thoughts, words and actions. We get out of life what we put into it.

Simple truths can sometimes be the most difficult to learn. Once you learn timeless lessons, you never forget them. Bobby and his big brother John certainly never have (says their proud mother).

Chapter 6: Friendship

Make new friends but keep the old,
One is silver and the other gold.
Girl Scouts of America

While I've known Barbara and Marcia the longest as sisters and close friends, I have other close friends, some I've known many years, some I met just recently. Other friends I don't feel close to yet I share interests and activities with. Andy and I have neighbors we were good friends with years ago, although we grew apart after one of us moved. We also have friends and former neighbors we still consider close friends even though we live miles apart and rarely, if ever, see each other or even talk on the phone.

In many ways, a close friendship, even a marriage, is paradoxical because it requires both individuals to respect boundaries—to remain close while remaining separate. In his timeless book, *The Prophet*, Kahlil Gibran says on the subject of marriage: " . . . let there be spaces in your togetherness." Even identical twins are different from each other. They have each other's backs, are similar in many ways, yet they are who they are with their own lives and ways of going and being. As I look back, all the friends who showed up in my life came at a time I needed them or they needed me, whether to have fun with, learn with, grieve with and grow with, either up and older, or both. Bottom line: no two friends are alike, "Unique as snowflakes, common as grass."

One friend I think of often who has since passed away introduced me to Father Richard Rohr, a Franciscan priest who founded the Center for Action and Contemplation in Albuquerque, NM. Father Richard introduced me to the Enneagram that's taught me more about who I am and why.

While today there are various definitions of the Enneagram, the first in-depth book I read about it is *The Enneagram: A Christian Perspective* by Richard Rohr and Andreas Ebert. Father Richard describes the Enneagram as an "ancient Christian tool for the discernment of spirits, the struggle with our capital sin, our 'false self,' and the encounter with our True Self in God."

Of the nine faces of God the Enneagram describes, I am definitely an Enneagram Two, born eager to please, eager to be accepted, needing continual reassurance I am loved for who I really am and not for who someone else wants me to be. I was also raised as a committed Christian who believed in God, and in Jesus the Son of God who taught us to follow his example. My parents taught me the importance of conscience, of having a moral compass to help me judge the difference between right and wrong and to act accordingly. Another word for this is integrity— walking your talk— having all your thoughts, words and actions in alignment. Jesus's main message, as I understood it, was: "Love the Lord your God with all your heart, your soul and your mind, and love your neighbor as yourself."

It was the loving myself part I had trouble with back then. Popular culture at the time made loving myself mean I was 'stuck up'. Nobody liked an arrogant stuck-up. I was also confused about the difference between loving others without giving myself away. I gave myself away too much in order to please and gain others' approval and friendship. In doing so, I sometimes compromised my values I later regretted.

Today, I am much more accepting of myself and those different from me than I was in my growing up years. Fortunately, my close friends today accept me as I am, and I accept them as they are. After 34 years of marriage, Andy and I realize that every day we have together we are learning with and from each other and will until we take our last breath. Even then, it's not the end. As another of my favorite teachers, Jesuit priest Pierre Teilhard de Chardin, said, "We are not human beings having a spiritual experience, we are spiritual beings having a human experience." In other words, we come from spirit and return to spirit after living a human life on Earth. Moreover, we not meant to make the journey from birth through life to death alone. We all need each other as we learn and grow together through the ups and downs of each and every day, with grace, gratitude, grit, forgiveness, humility and humor.

Chapter 7: Once in a Lifetime

Unique as snowflakes, common as grass.
—Unknown

Have you ever lived through a *once-in-a-lifetime* experience you agreed to before doing it; one that revealed something priceless you've never forgotten? For me, this was an overnight field trip in Northern Michigan with the Michigan Audubon Society. Skeptical when my friend invited me to join her, she assured me it would be an unforgettable experience. We were instructed to bring a sack lunch, bottled water, tarp and sleeping bag, flashlight and cross-country skis. While the Michigan Biological Station near Pellston had a beautiful lodge, with restrooms, a kitchen and a large, wood burning fireplace, our group of about 30 wouldn't be sleeping in the lodge. We would be sleeping in snow igloos we ourselves would make somewhere away from the lodge, in the surrounding woods.

Once we arrived, we were told how the day would unfold: First, we would break up into groups of two, pile up mounds of snow to make igloos, enjoy a guided bird-watching tour through the woods on cross-country skis, carve out our igloos before going to the lodge for dinner followed by a lecture about birds before turning in for the night.

Fortunately, the day started out with sunshine and blue skies, so the drive north from Petoskey to Pellston was pleasant, with no more snow or storms on the horizon. Once we arrived at our destination, we got out of our warm car all bundled up from head to foot in outdoor wear. Right away, taking in my first breath of fresh air, I knew it would be a very, very cold night. Having lived in northern Michigan for more than 10 years, with 190 inches of snow the first year we moved there from Ohio, I was used to winter weather. Still, I had never been so intimately exposed to it for so long, and, at times, up to my knees.

We were instructed to work in pairs to amass a huge pile of snow, to pack it down firmly and large enough to hold two sleeping bags, two people, and whatever small, items we couldn't do without for an overnight. After everyone's huge mound of snow had passed muster with our leader, we came together to go cross-country skiing through the woods. Everything around us was snow-covered and sparkling from rays of sunshine coming down through the trees, as our leader described the genus and species of birds flitting through the branches, chirping away with their own unique songs. After coming back to camp, we were instructed to dig out our igloos and spread out our tarp and sleeping bags so we would be ready to crawl in for the night when the time came.

Following dinner there was a lecture about birds native to Northern Michigan. Afterwards, we sat around and talked about our day while looking through a number of large picture books on nature. One book was filled with nothing but close-up photographs of snowflakes, page after page of snowflakes, every one unique, absolutely gorgeous, like precious, one-of-a-kind crystals created by master artists. While I don't remember the title of the book, the writer, photographer or publisher, I will always remember what I learned by looking through page after page and reading about where snowflakes come from and where they go after they melt, back from where they came. We humans are like snowflakes, no two alike, brief lifespan, delicate when alone, powerful when together, common as grass.

That night, it was so cold inside my sleeping bag even with all my indoor *and* outdoor clothes on, I didn't sleep much. Maybe I dozed off for a half-hour or so here and there, but all I could do in the meantime was pray I wouldn't have to relieve myself and for morning to come sooner rather than later. Eventually it did, and everyone emerged from their igloos to enjoy a hearty breakfast together in the lodge before we packed up and drove back home.

After Googling the word snowflake, I learned a snowflake's shape evolves as it journeys through the air. Even two flakes floating side by side will be blown through different levels of humidity and vapor to create a truly unique shape. Reflecting back on that camping trip 40 years ago, I am grateful I did it when I was younger. One of the most valuable lessons I've ever learned is that with a strong and steady faith, we'll discover there's a gift in every dark side and a dark side in every gift, even in *once-in-a-lifetime* experiences.

Chapter 8: Compete *and* Create!
Imagination and curiosity should be at the center of your life.
—Ray Bradbury

When I found myself single again after being a full-time mother and homemaker for 13 years, I had to find a way to support myself and provide what I could for my sons. An ad that appeared in our local newspaper caught my eye: "Interested in running your own business? Do you have secretarial skills? Call Swaby, Cormican & Wise Realtors, 347-1780." After my first interview, I landed a job as a 'Girl Friday' for the firm's three partners. They paid me $400 a month to answer their phone, type up closing statements and greet their clients and potential clients who came in the door.

In exchange for 40 percent of my 40-hour week, they told me I could use their telephone, copy machine and typewriter 60 percent of my week to provide secretarial services for other clients. Even so, they expected me to remain in the office the full 40 hours a week to answer their phone, greet their clients and type up closing statements. Thus, I established myself as a sole proprietorship, and Swaby, Cormican and Wise became my first clients.

Admittedly, I was curious to see if I had what it took to be a business owner, like my dad. Initially, things went better than expected and within a year or two, I had to hire three additional staff, took over the majority of the real estate's office space, purchased my own 40K RadioShack computer, learned list management, and eventually offered mass mailing in additional to secretarial and accounting services. Professional Business Services was launched and thriving.

This was in the early 1980s, in Petoskey, Michigan. As the only such service in town, business was brisk with no competition for clients. My confidence improved once I was able to pay my bills with some left over for incidentals and savings. One day, an attractive and confident young woman walked into my office, introduced herself and said she was moving to Petoskey and wanted to start her own secretarial service. She asked how I got started, how I acquired new clients, even how much I charged per word for transcribing.

At first, I felt some resistance to telling her how I got started for fear she might put me out of business. She seemed more confident than I had been when I struck out on my own. I told her I didn't have time to talk just then, so we arranged to meet for coffee the next day. That evening, I thought about what I would share with her. I remembered what my dad told me when he started his wholesale construction equipment business in 1946 in Columbus, Ohio, "Competitors make us better. Compete fair and square by distinguishing yourself from your competition with your own brand of quality and service customers can count on." Daddy's business slogan was 'Equipment of Merit'. He always told my sisters and me what mattered most was how you treat your customers *after* the sale. The next day, I gave this woman the same price list I handed out to potential clients. Assuring her she would attract clients who needed her unique skills just as I did, we parted as friendly colleagues.

Eventually, she did well and I ended up with more business than I could handle. Still, I began to wonder if my 'ladder to success' was against the wrong wall. Was I trying to be like my father since I was no longer a full-time mother—my first priority when my sons were born? Was I pretending to love being 'the boss' when I didn't want to be anyone's boss. Instead, I was a dreamer who wanted to be a writer. To extinguish such thoughts, I considered them fiction rather than fact. In a last minute attempt to succeed in the mailing business, I took in a partner with impressive downstate street savvy, hoping she would become the head of the business so I could be the heart. Together, I hoped and prayed, we would grow the business as a team.

Unfortunately, her way of dealing with customers didn't align with mine. Within six months, I called my attorney and sold my half of the business to her, took a job as manager of a kitchen design studio in Grand Rapids, packed up all my belongings, said good-bye to my two sons, longtime friends and neighbors and started all over again. Little did I know at the time that my dream of becoming a real writer would soon become a reality in a way I could never imagine, not in a million years.

Chapter 9: Thank you, Mr. Imbs!

*If the only prayer you ever say in your entire life
is thank you, it will be enough!*
—Meister Eckhart

After the Walloon Lake Association (WLA) hired me to be their executive secretary in the early 1980s, I worked with many accomplished individuals from around the country. Back then, personal wealth of residents vacationing during the summer months within a five-mile radius of Little Traverse Bay of Lake Michigan, encompassing Petoskey, Harbor Springs, Charlevoix and Boyne City, was said to be the most sizable of anywhere in the world. Family names such as Ford, Fisher, Gamble, Swift, Armour, Wrigley and Wilson representing some of the most nationally and internationally recognizable brand names from automobiles to chewing gum were among the most well known property owners of summer residences.

One of the not-so-well-known names was Imbs—Joseph Francis Imbs II—who owned a summer home on Walloon Lake. I had never met Mr. Imbs, but I knew he was a WLA member and had heard about him. Other Wallooners told me Mr. Imbs's personal wealth was impressive because he invented cake mixes. Cake mixes were very popular then as they are now. To think a Wallooner could claim such an achievement was awe-inspiring to me.

One morning, a slightly built and modestly dressed man walked into my office in downtown Petoskey. He approached my desk with a pleasant smile and an extended hand.

"Good morning," he said. "My name is Joe Imbs. I'm pleased to meet you."

I stood, shook his hand, and told him it was an honor to meet him. He said he had stopped by to meet me and to pick up a few extra copies of *The Wallooner,* our monthly summer magazine.

After chatting with him a few minutes, I felt comfortable enough to ask him a question. As sole proprietor of Professional Businesses

Services, I told him I was always looking for ways to grow my fledgling business.

"I've heard you've been very successful, Mr. Imbs. To what do you attribute your success?"

Surprised by my question, he smiled, paused briefly, then said, "I think it's because I never forgot to thank everyone who helped me along the way."

Mr. Imbs' honest response felt like a validation of my own values that had been threatened at times. As a single woman trying to achieve success in a man's world, I quickly learned being nice didn't pay the bills. Being tough did, but it wasn't my nature to be tough. Mr. Imbs helped me realize it's possible to be both tough and tender at the same time, while staying true to values of appreciation, humility, integrity, and kindness. I never did ask him if he invented cake mixes but I was able to locate his obituary on-line in *The St. Louis Post-Dispatch.*

It turns out Mr. Imbs was the third generation of his family to become president and CEO of the J.F. Imbs Milling Company, which later merged with Nebraska Consolidated Mills, to become today's ConAgra Brands (NYSE: CAG). Mr. Imbs was described as a gentleman and thoughtful friend, a man remembered for his smile and the twinkle in his eye, dearly missed by all who had the good fortune of making his acquaintance. I felt honored to be one of them.

So, thank you, Mr. Imbs, for reinforcing for me the importance of saying thank you. Thank you for reminding me that doing so benefits the one saying thank-you, as well as the one being thanked. Everyone appreciates being appreciated.

Chapter 9: The Road Not Taken

Two roads diverged in the yellow woods,
And sorry I could not travel both
And be one traveler, long I stood
And looked down one as far as I could
To where it bent in the undergrowth;
—Ralph Waldo Emerson

The year I turned 37, I found myself at a formidable crossroads. For inspiration, I taped a copy of Emerson's familiar poem, *The Road Not Taken*, to my refrigerator. I read it over and over again as I pondered its sobering message. Once I started down one road, I knew I would never come back to where I had begun. My 14-year marriage was about to end, and with two young sons to raise, ages 11 and 8, my future looked bleak.

A poetry lover all my life, I memorized Frost's classic as a constant reminder that I, too, would find the wisdom when the time came to choose the best road to travel. I didn't want my sons to feel responsible for the breakup of their parents' marriage because they weren't. During the early months of 1980 when such thoughts dominated my waking hours, I never imagined how far away I would eventually travel to discover the true meaning of 'home'.

Up to this point, I had enjoyed a near-idyllic life that my parents, my religion, and my culture had taught me to live. Now nearing my 40th birthday in the late 1970s, I was feeling adrift. Facing challenges I wasn't prepared for, I was more disheartened because I didn't know why. It was then that my faith came alive for me after I got out the Bible my Grandmother Harman gave me for Christmas when I was eight, and started reading it for the first time.

My life went on, of course, and my Bible and Frost's poem went with me. After selling my business in Petoskey, I accepted a new job in Grand Rapids, although my boys would stay in Petoskey with their father and stepmother. I had to trust that I was making the right decisions for the right reasons, for them and for me. I couldn't envision how my future, or theirs, would unfold, but I knew I wanted someday to marry a man who shared my values and dreams for a real home together with our families.

When Andy Daugavietis proposed marriage on September 11, 1988, it seemed my dream was beginning to come true. We had dated for five years, even though I now lived and worked in Grand Rapids, Michigan. He still practiced medicine at Burns Clinic in Petoskey and his son Peter would soon graduate from Petoskey High School. His daughter Leis lived in Tallahassee, Florida with her mother and was a junior at Leon High School. My sons John and Bob lived with their dad and Bridget, their stepmother, in Petoskey. John was a freshman at Hillsdale College and Bob was a junior at Petoskey High School.

What I had not expected was Andy calling two weeks later to tell me he had a job offer in Riyadh, Saudi Arabia. I knew he had received an offer six months earlier from King Faisal Hospital in Riyadh, but he couldn't get his affairs in order in time to accept the position. I was mistaken when I assumed that would be the end of his desire for a mid-life adventure in the Middle East.

"The mail just came," he said excitedly. "King Fahad National Guard Hospital is offering me a two-year contract as a senior staff consultant in rheumatology. If I accept, I have to report to work on January 10th."

"Andy, that's only four months from today."

"Yes, isn't it great? Should we accept?"

I took a deep breath, then heard myself say, "Yes, let's go."

-o0o-

My decision to marry Andy and go with him to Saudi Arabia was the most difficult decision I ever made; yet, it was the best decision I ever made. I came to understand the power of paradox to change my dualistic 'either/or' thinking to non-dual 'both/and' thinking. Meeting people from around the world taught me the value of diversity. I learned to accept other cultures, religions, ethnicities and traditions as interesting rather than reasons to be fearful of those different from me. I learned that first impressions aren't always accurate. I learned that real heroes are those who reach across false boundaries that divide us as humans to show selfless courage in times of crisis and uncertainty. I also learned I had more courage, more confidence, more compassion for others and myself than I ever realized.

I learned my story is not all about me. My story is also Our Story, shared with girls and women around the world who are taught to believe they are 'less than' men. I've learned that people of color have their story, and those whose sexuality and gender identity differ from male and female have their story, too.

All of our stories are part of The Story of humanity—the story that all of us are created to be who we are and sustained in that authenticity by the same loving and omnipotent God that created the Universe. We breathe the same air; we drink the same water. We all depend on the same Sun to warm our planet and grow our food. We all need the love of family and friends to live lives of meaning and purpose. I truly believe we also have the ability, if we can muster the collective will, to someday write the story of how we, as inhabitants of the same planet, came together as One, during this critical time in history, to create a world that works for everyone.

Even though some experiences I had in Saudi Arabia were painful, I now see everything that happened more than 25 years ago from a positive perspective. I can look back on what occurred before, during and after our time in the Middle East with forgiveness and humor. I rediscovered my love of writing, especially real stories about real people who make a positive difference in the lives of others. I learned to 'lighten up' and quit taking myself so seriously. I learned that every human life born into our world has intrinsic potential and divine power for good. I learned that thoughts lead us to choices that create our reality, personally and collectively, by what we choose to think and how we choose to live.

Chapter 11: Dr. Judith

Open your mind to the world and the many different ways that can be found in it before making hasty judgments of others.
—C. Joybell C.

Although it's been 30 years since Andy and I lived in Saudi Arabia, more than a few individuals I met there made lasting impressions on me and taught me timeless lessons. Dr. Judith Finlayson is one of them.

In the spring issue the hospital's monthly magazine the focus was on nursing. As the first female ever hired to be a writer for the Public Affairs Department, I was pleased to be assigned the lead article on nursing and the first physician profile featuring a female—Dr. Judith Finlayson, a primary care physician from Canada, married to a neurosurgeon at King Fahad. Dr. Judith, as she was referred to by staff members, was also my personal physician at King Fahad,

"Growing up in Australia, I was taught that anyone different wasn't desirable," she said. "From my own travels and experiences I now know people are much the same all over the world. Prejudice and hostility are a result of fear about other people you don't know. Living in Saudi Arabia is a lesson in getting on together regardless of culture and religion. Instead of, 'How peculiar,' I say, 'How interesting.'"

When I asked for her most memorable experience as a physician in Saudi Arabia, she told me about a male patient, a general in the Saudi Arabian National Guard.

"His diet was lacking in bulk and fiber. I prescribed a kilo of prunes everyday and told him to come back to see me in a month. When he returned, he was elated. He said he was 'cured'—a changed man. In fact, he ordered a daily supply of prunes for all the soldiers in the field."

While the first part of Judith's story was amusing, the second part of her story was astounding.

"The general told me he planned to host a gala dinner in my honor at his palace. My husband and I and as many guests as I wanted to include were invited. Andrew and I, our son, and good friends, Jean and Ramsey, were chauffeured by limousine to the general's palace in Rawdah, an exclusive area of Riyadh. Once we arrived, the men were escorted through one door of the palace and Jean and I were shown through another entrance that led to the harem—the women's quarters.

"She and I were served tea, cookies and dates as we sat for three and a half hours looking at party dresses modeled for us by the younger ladies, eating dates and cookies and drinking tea."

Finally, nearing midnight, a male servant summoned Judith and Jean into the dining room, now empty of male guests. The two of them were given plates and told to help themselves to leftovers on the buffet tables.

"After Jean and I finished eating, the general came into the dining room to thank me again and say goodnight. He told me he announced to the prominent guests gathered at dinner that evening that he was indebted to me for curing him of a lifelong ailment. Our husbands and my son joined us and the limousine came and took us back home."

Although she was excluded from attending the banquet in her honor, Judith wasn't offended by the cultural differences. When asked to name a person who exemplified her ideal figure, she said, "Mahatma Gandhi."

In his book, *The 8 Laws of Change: How To Be An Agent of Personal And Social Transformation*, Stephan A. Schwartz tells how Gandhi answered a reporter's question in New Delhi shortly before Gandhi was assassinated in 1948. When the reporter asked what he had done to force the British to leave India after centuries of domination, Gandhi said, "It was the nature of our character that caused the British to leave India."

Schwartz goes on to say, "The secret to non-violent social transformation is based on choice, exercised every day, throughout the day. Usually it's a small moment of decision in which, of the options available, one of the most compassionate and life-affirming."

Yes, Dr. Judith made a lasting impression on me in just one in-depth interview with her 30 years ago, confirmed by Schwartz's book now a permanent addition to my personal library. I wish I could thank both of them for reminding me to also see others who are different as "interesting" rather than 'evil', bad or wrong, a disturbing and increasingly prevalent point-of-view in today's either/or, my-way-or-the-highway politically, culturally, and religiously divided world.

Chapter 12: *Inshallah*[3]—God Willing
You get out of life what you put into it.
—Marianne Alireza

An audible gasp filled the room as American-born Marianne Alireza strode to the podium. Smiling and waving, she wore a glittering, shimmering, full-length, red-silk cape trimmed with 24k-gold embroidery. Grasping both sides of the collar, she removed the cape with a flourish to reveal an elegant, full-length red silk gown, studded generously with rubies and emeralds. She waved and smiled at the audience of 200 American female expats who responded by giving her a standing ovation. I, too, couldn't contain my excitement and stood with the others as we cheered and clapped. Beaming with appreciation, she motioned for us to sit and quiet down. She knew very well why we had come to hear her speak. She was one of us, an American woman who followed the man she loved to Saudi Arabia.

Marianne moved to Riyadh in 1944 with her baby daughter and her husband, Ali Alireza, the first Saudi national to attend college in the U.S. The two met at the University of California at Berkley in 1941. Everyone wanted to know how she was able to come to Saudi Arabia to live before automobiles, grocery stores, air conditioning and running water. The Arabia Mrs. Alireza came to was exotic and primitive—a land of sheiks, camel caravans, incense and slaves. She lived in mud palaces, while all of us were living in marble villas furnished with air conditioners, telephones, flush toilets you could sit on, washers and dryers.

"It was like living in the Old Testament times," she said. "Camels were the main mode of transportation. There were no medical facilities, no plumbing or electricity. When you got sick, you either got well on your own or you died. It was that simple."

Mrs. Alireza's descriptions of Saudi Arabia in the late 1940s piqued my curiosity, but they didn't hold as much intrigue as how she survived excruciating homesickness, the loss of personal freedom and intense

---

[3] If God wills it.

culture shock. I had struggled with all these feelings myself. I wanted to learn all I could from this amazing woman with the hope that it would help me make the most of my remaining months in Saudi Arabia and feel more confident about being here myself.

Mrs. Alireza said her first meeting with her mother-in-law bonded the two women for life. She described how welcoming it was when Ali's mother greeted her with a warm embrace and told her she loved her, just as she loved her son.

"My first Christmas in Saudi Arabia, my mother-in-law arranged to have a real Christmas tree flown in from Cairo. It was complete with decorations and lighted candles. There were gifts under the tree and a stuffed turkey with all the trimmings for dinner," she said.

"Few in Saudi Arabia had a frame of reference to know who I was or where I came from. You could count on one hand the number of Saudi nationals who knew what was going on in the world beyond the next village. Somehow, Ali's mother knew about Christmas, but she didn't understand it completely. For every other special occasion throughout the year, including my daughter's first birthday, a Christmas tree miraculously appeared in our home, out of nowhere."

Within months of her arrival in the Kingdom, Mrs. Alireza developed a fever she later believed to be strep throat. With no Western doctors to treat her, the women of the harem covered her body with wet compresses while a slave girl fanned her with an ostrich plume.

"It was my own determination, and God's will, that enabled me to survive," she said.

Within hours after she was back on her feet, word came that King Abdul Aziz wanted to meet her. Escorted to the reception room, she waited sitting cross-legged with other veiled women who had been called for the royal visit. Once the King appeared, he made his way around the room greeting each female and sharing a brief conversation in Arabic.

"I was numb from the waist down, unaccustomed to sitting in that position for such a long time, and still weak from my illness," Mrs. Alireza said. "I amused myself by watching as the other women spoke, their veils moving in and out with each puff of breath. I got a giggle fit because it was so humorous to watch—probably a combination of nervous apprehension and disbelief that I was about to meet the King for the first time."

Suddenly, King Abdul Aziz, the legendary hero of Saudi Arabia, stood two feet away. He wore the customary red-and-white checked ghutra and a gold-trimmed black cape over his white thobe.

"He looked larger than life," said Mrs. Alireza. "I rose to my feet with great difficulty on legs that felt strangely detached from my body."

While Mrs. Alireza's college degree was in languages, Arabic wasn't one of them. She uttered the only word she knew that means 'hello'.

"Marhaba," she said, as she turned to walk away.

The Saudi ruler wasn't done with her yet. In a booming voice, the King spoke again and waited for her reply. Mrs. Alireza had no idea what he said, only that he wanted an answer. Frantic to say something—anything—she repeated a word uttered numerous times over her feverish body by the women of the harem.

"Inshallah," she said, to the obvious pleasure of the King, who nodded and disappeared from the room.

Mrs. Alireza was more willing to use a word she didn't know rather than to remain silent. When she told her husband of her brief conversation with the King, Ali was greatly amused and proud of his American-born, non-Arabic-speaking wife. The King asked Mrs. Alireza, a Christian, if she would convert to Islam. Her response, meaning 'if God wills it', satisfied the King's curiosity and gained his approval.

Describing the day her husband's brother telephoned to inform her that Ali had divorced her and taken another wife, Mrs. Alireza became emotional for the first and only time during her talk. Although she didn't reveal when Ali divorced her, where she was at the time, or what she was doing, she said her first fear was for their five children. They were all older than seven years of age and in school in Switzerland. Saudi law gave the husband full custody of children older than seven. Mrs. Alireza said details of the divorce and ensuing conflicts over custody were revealed in her book, *At the Drop of a Veil.* Her husband had the book banned from the Kingdom before his death in the late 1970s. Eventually, she reunited with her children. Prior to his death, she and Ali worked out an amicable visitation schedule. When they grew to adulthood, all of the children chose to live in Saudi Arabia. Mrs. Alireza never remarried, and she never became a Muslim. Only her close relationship with King Faisal, assassinated in July of 1958, made it possible for her to enter the Kingdom to visit her grown children. News of her arrival in Riyadh for her appearance at the American Embassy never made local newspapers. If the mutawa[4] had learned of her visit, there would have been trouble, even though the Embassy was off limits to them.

Following her talk, I walked up to the podium to shake her hand. I felt a kinship with this woman, a Christian who came to Saudi Arabia because she loved her husband. Once here, in spite of the losses, hardships, and adjustments, she learned acceptance and forgiveness, lessons I was still learning.

"If you could distill all you learned by firsthand experience in Saudi Arabia, what would your best advice?" I asked.

"You get out of life what you put into it," she said. "No matter what happens to you, life goes on. When I was growing up in Oklahoma, nobody traveled or knew what was going on in the world. I am fortunate to have learned through firsthand experience. Knowledge and understanding bring wisdom. We need more wisdom in our world today."

Her words captivated me. I was seeing and hearing a real-life example of the kind of person I wanted to be. Her heart had been broken, and her family separated physically, yet they had remained close in spirit. She learned to forgive her husband and by doing so gained more than she lost. She became a better citizen of the world.

"Only Ali divorced me. My Arabian family didn't divorce me. We proved that even if you come from worlds apart, you can still have mutual love, respect, and tolerance. The compensation for the disappointments has been the people I have grown to love and who love me. They have made all the difference."

----

[4] A member of the religious police in Saudi Arabia

Chapter 13: Emmanuel

*We are absolutely grounded in the love of God
that protects us from nothing, even as
it sustains us in all things.*
—James Finley

On my first day back to work after vacation, I was sad to learn that
Emmanuel, our Public Affairs photographer, was a patient in King Fahad
Hospital. My heart sank when Nabiha told me he had a malignant brain
tumor. Surgery to remove the tumor had not been successful. We all
loved Emmanuel—a quiet yet friendly man, a hard worker, a talented
photographer and always punctual. He was married, the father of five
children in Nigeria. He was also a Christian.

By the time I found out about Emmanuel's illness, doctors had done
all they could to get him strong enough to go home. He wanted so badly
to see his family before he died, but that was not to be. As a Christian, I
had to go to Emmanuel and offer whatever support I could. Nabiha said
Emmanuel was frightened and depressed about dying. King Fahad
Hospital had no official Christian pastors on staff to support him in his
faith. It was up to each of us, as Christians, to do what we felt moved to
do, discretely, in our own way, on our own time, to help him.

When I walked into his room, I sat in a chair next to his bed and
waited to see if he was awake. His eyes were closed and he was
breathing heavily. His head was wrapped entirely in bandages. He was
propped up on pillows and his hands were clasped together on his chest
as if praying.

"Emmanuel," I whispered, not wanting to startle or awaken him.
Slowly he opened his eyes, looked at me and smiled. He was weak and
lethargic, but I could tell he was happy to see me. I nodded and smiled at
him and then decided to share some thoughts with him about death and
dying from my perspective.

"Emmanuel, I brought my Bible to work today, but you're the only
one who knows this." He smiled, closed his eyes and nodded.

"I've never been in your situation so I can't say I know how you feel. I know my heart is breaking for you, and I know I would want somebody to affirm my faith for me and with me if I were you."

Witnessing my faith to others was not something I had much practice with or felt comfortable doing. I had never read from the Bible to a dying person. Even though as a child I attended Sunday School faithfully for years and learned all about Jesus and His life, death and resurrection, I was not taught to voice aloud what I believed and why.

I began reading at verse 1, Chapter 5 of St. Matthew in the New Testament and read through verse 18, the Beatitudes from the Sermon on the Mount. This passage had always been a favorite of mine. I was hoping it would comfort Emmanuel, too. I stopped reading, saw Emmanuel was weeping, and I reached for his hand.

"It's okay," he said. "I always loved the Beatitudes. May I ask a question?"

"Yes, of course."

"Do you believe I'll go to heaven when I die and that Jesus will watch over my family after I'm gone?"

"Yes, I do, Emmanuel. In Sunday school, I was taught that your name 'Emmanuel' means 'God with us.' Your name and your baptism assure you that He is with you and your family—always. I also believe what the Bible says about life after death, and that death only takes the body. Your spirit or soul is eternal. I believe Jesus will come for you at the time of your death, and you will know He is here. He is here with you now, with us, right now, today. After we die, because of Jesus Christ, our soul lives forever with God and in the hearts and memories of those we loved and who loved us."

I had not planned to say what I said, and I worried I had said too much. Emmanuel closed his eyes again. I waited a few moments, trying to decide if I should leave or stay. I decided to say goodbye and come again the next day.

"Emmanuel," I said softly, "I'm leaving now. I'll be back again tomorrow. I want you to know I'll write to your wife and family and tell them how much we love and respect you in Public Affairs. I'll also tell them I came to visit you and that you're not alone here—that your Christian friends are looking after you and praying for you. I'll tell them your faith is strong and that you're being brave and courageous in spite of your illness."

When I came the next day, the nurse told me Emmanuel had slipped into a coma. The doctors prescribed a sedative after he complained of pain. I visited Emmanuel two more times, but only to stand by his bed and say a prayer for him and his family. We never spoke again, but the last time I visited him, I noticed the worry lines across his forehead and around his mouth had disappeared. Emmanuel looked peaceful and ready to go. He died the following day.

My time with Emmanuel opened my eyes to a new awareness of how strong my faith was even though I had never expressed my beliefs so openly before. Growing up, we always prayed before meals and bedtime, yet my parents never spoke about what they believed and why. I couldn't recall hearing them talk about their doubts and fears regarding faith, or asking us if we had questions about theological matters. Emmanuel gave me a greater gift than I had given him by being the strong and faithful Christian he was, even at a time when he was frightened, suffering physically, and missing his family and home.

Chapter 14: Going Home

*A person travels the world in search of what
s/he needs and returns home to find it.*
—George Moore, Irish novelist (1852-1933)

On our day of departure, I awoke with mixed emotions. I felt joyful
excitement, nervous anxiety, and, yes, sadness, too. As obsessively as I
had counted the days before we could leave, I was surprised by my
sentimental mood. I walked through all the empty rooms in our villa,
pausing to recall memories from our first day here. I was a new bride
then, a new stepmother, a middle-aged woman in search of herself, who
also found in the Arabian Desert happiness, adventure, friendships, and
the beginnings of a career as a writer. I gazed out the windows at our
neighborhood, knowing I would never come back to this place again. I
wanted always to remember this special time Andy and I shared together
as husband and wife, but I couldn't wait to get home to our children, our
families, and to our real lives in America.

Our plane was scheduled to leave Riyadh at 9:45 p.m. We had been
advised to leave our keys on the kitchen counter and lock our villa when
we left for the airport. It was 6:45 p.m. when the limousine pulled in
front of our villa, and we closed the door for the last time. At that
moment, we were homeless and without passports. A fellow named
Abdullah in staff services told us Mohammed would meet us at the
airport with our passports, standard operating procedure for departing
expats. We were naive to believe him.

Chaos greeted us at the airport. I had never seen such a diverse mass
of humanity in one place or heard such clamor—people yelling, babies
crying, announcements blaring over the loud speaker in Arabic. Before
us were the fleeing citizenry of Riyadh—countless men, non-Saudi
Middle Easterners for the most part, wearing turbans and carrying boxes
and soft bundles tied together with rope, veiled females carrying babies,
small children carrying blankets and holding hands, all with terrified
looks on their faces, many in tears.

We scanned the crowd for Mohammed. Abdullah said he would be waiting for us near the Saudia ticket counter. Andy stood five feet away from where I waited with our bags, looking for the man who held our very lives in his hands. Without our passports, we couldn't check in. If we didn't check in soon, we wouldn't leave. I watched the minute hands on the clock overhead move from 8:00 to 8:15 to 8:30. Still no sign of Mohammed.

"Andy, call Administration. Call someone. Find Mohammed," I shouted loudly enough for Andy to hear me above all the commotion. "If we don't get those passports, we're not getting out of here."

Andy hurried to a nearby pay phone. I continued to watch for Mohammed as Andy called the hospital. When I glanced over to see if he was able to reach anyone, his grim expression crushed my hopes. All I could do was close my eyes and pray.

Dear God, thank you for bringing us this far. We must leave tonight, or we won't get out before the war. Many others also want to be on that plane when it leaves. Please get all of us out safely.

"The guy I spoke with said Mohammed should have been here half an hour ago," Andy said when he came back.

We stood by our luggage in silence, helpless to do anything but wait. I was too angry to cry. Fifteen anxious minutes later, here comes Mohammed, sauntering aimlessly through the crowd, grinning from ear to ear. Without apology, explanation or sense of urgency, he handed over our passports. I have never been so happy to hold such a small, yet so essential, object in my hands. Relieved beyond words, I simply smiled at Mohammed. Andy thanked him in Arabic and shook his hand. We gathered our bags and hurried to the end of the line in front of the Saudia check-in counter.

"You'll have to hurry. The plane is full," the agent said. "No seat assignments."

We grabbed our carry-ons and ran as fast as we could without bumping into other passengers making their way to the departure gate. Once up the stairs and through the front entrance of the 747, it was a free-for-all. People were elbowing each other to get seats together. We spotted two empty seats by a window in the rear of the economy section and made a dash to claim them. Within minutes, all seats in our cabin were taken. In the row across the aisle from us sat two U.S. soldiers, young fellows going on leave.

"Thank you for your service," Andy said as he reached over to shake hands with both of them.

I was so emotional I couldn't speak. I waved and smiled instead. I thought of John and Bob and how glad I was they weren't wearing military uniforms and preparing to fight in any wars. In the row in front of the soldiers sat four Saudi females, all veiled, all holding infants and toddlers crying loudly and inconsolably.

"This may be a long ride," I said to Andy.

Once airborne, we expected to touch down in Jeddah, as before, and then on to New York. We knew the plane was full, but perhaps some of the passengers would get out in Jeddah and others would board. Not so. The pilot announced we were carrying an unusually heavy load—more passengers and cargo than ever before. Thus, we would have only a brief layover in London to refuel, but we were not to leave the plane. He also told us King Khalid Airport closed after we left. Jean was right. The U.S. finally declared a travel advisory.

Andy settled back in his seat to sleep. I couldn't stop thinking about the chaos we had just escaped, and how grateful I was that we were leaving. I prayed for those left behind, for a safe flight ahead, and for war in the Middle East to be avoided. I thought about seeing John and Bob again, my mother and everyone else who had written so faithfully while we were away. It broke my heart to have to burn every piece of mail we had received before we left. We couldn't fit it in our suitcases or carry-ons. I kept a few letters from the boys and watched the rest of the dozens of cards and letters go up in flames and smoke in the stone-covered courtyard behind our villa.

With a long flight ahead of us, I pulled out *The Road from Coorain* by Jill Ker Conway the book my Canadian friend Rosemary gave me, turned on my overhead light, and settled back in my seat. I had no prior knowledge of Jill Ker Conway, and quickly learned she left her home in

Australia to later become the first female president of Smith College. After finishing the first chapter, I couldn't put the book down. Throughout the flight, I continued to read between meals, dozing off occasionally for an hour or so at a time.

Reading Conway's memoir caused me to reflect on my own journey from Worthington, Ohio, to Petoskey, Michigan, to Grand Rapids, Michigan, back to Petoskey, and then to Saudi Arabia and now back to Michigan. A decade ago, I thought my life was over. Now, I truly believed my life was just beginning.

As our plane approached J.F.K., I was so emotional I couldn't stop crying. We flew over New York Harbor and saw the Statue of Liberty, the twin towers of the World Trade Center and the Empire State Building. Along with everyone else on board, Andy and I could hardly contain our emotions. Passengers cheered as they strained to look out the windows while staying strapped in their seats. The moment the wheels of our 747 touched down on the runway, passengers erupted in shouts of joy and clapping. I had never felt so patriotic as when we landed in New York that day. I couldn't wait to touch the ground once we disembarked. The babies across the aisle were crying at the top of their lungs. Their mothers were hurriedly gathering up their belongings. We had been on that plane, in our seats, for nearly 18 hours. Once in the international terminal, we only had a few minutes to make one phone call each before claiming our luggage and catching a bus to La Guardia. I called Mother and Andy called his parents. It was 10:00 a.m.

"Mother, we're in New York," I said the minute she picked up the phone. "We're safe. It is so good to hear your voice."

"Pammy, I'm so relieved. How soon do you leave for Grand Rapids?"

"Our plane leaves La Guardia around 1:00. We make a quick stop in Detroit and should be in Grand Rapids by 4:00 this afternoon. I'll call you as soon as we get to Grand Haven."

The soldiers who sat behind us were waiting for their bags when we got to baggage claim. We overheard them complaining about the babies wailing all the way from Riyadh. Perhaps past experience with our own babies made it easier for us to tune out their familiar cries.

"I'm never getting married," said one soldier. "I'm never having kids," said another. I have often thought of those young fellows, wondering if they ever changed their minds.

The remainder of our long journey home was uneventful. Andy's parents and sister Anita met us at the airport in Grand Rapids. We had been traveling for nearly 27 hours—from the time we left our villa to the time we walked in the front door of Andy's parents' home in Grand Haven. I called Mother first, and then the boys in Hillsdale.

That night in bed, as Andy slept next to me, I couldn't stop thinking about those we left behind, friends and colleagues at the hospital, neighbors on Al Awzae, friends in the writer's group. I thanked God we made it home safely, grateful we had talked with all our kids that day, our parents and siblings. I tried to think of happier, more peaceful times to come—like seeing our kids and family on a more regular basis. We had missed them all and wanted to reconnect with everyone as soon as possible. So many changes had taken place in the interim, in all our lives.

If only we can avoid war, inshallah, inshallah, inshallah, I kept repeating over and over to myself until I eventually surrendered into a deep, and blessed, sleep.

Chapter 15: P.S. I Love You

A tree's beauty lies in its branches,
but its strength lies in its roots.
Matshona Dhliwayo[5]

One morning shortly after Andy and I returned home from Saudi Arabia, I was watching the TODAY Show when author Dorothy Rich appeared as a guest. I had never heard of Dorothy Rich, but was interested in what she had to say about children in the U.S. When we were in Riyadh, I couldn't follow U.S. news as closely as I wanted to because there was no TV. The only credible news we could get was on BBC[6] radio. Now that we were home, I couldn't stop watching televised news, especially with the Gulf War underway, the war we had escaped by only a week.

Dorothy was an educator and author who helped champion the idea that parental involvement can make a significant difference in a child's education. She was promoting her book published in 1988, titled, *MegaSkills: How Families Help Children Succeed in School and Beyond.* During the interview, she said she wrote the book because of her concerns about how college admissions SAT and ACT test scores were dropping, and how kindergarten and first grade teachers were concerned because children weren't coming to school ready to learn. The reason? Dorothy said they lacked self-regulating skills, defined in Wikipedia as "the ability to understand and manage your behavior and reactions to feelings and things happening around you, including reactions to strong emotions like frustration, excitement, anger and embarrassment." After earning her PhD in education from Catholic University, Dorothy, a former public school teacher herself, founded the Washington-based Home and School Institute in the 1960s. She said she wanted to be part of a movement to get parents across the country willing to stand shoulder

---

[5] Matshona Dhliwayo is a Canadian based Philosopher, Entrepreneur, and author of books such as *The Little Book of Inspiration, Creativity, The Book, 50 Lessons Every Wise Mother Teaches Her Son, 100 Lessons Every Great Man Wants You to Know*, and *Lalibela's Wise Man.*

[6] British Broadcasting Radio

to shoulder with teachers to ensure that our children have the best possible education.

"No matter how many changes are made in school, even more significant support and change need to come from the homes from which students come to school," she said. "That's what brings about real and sustained educational reform."

Right way, I ordered a copy of Dorothy's book and arranged for her to come to Grand Rapids to promote her book, which she did. While that was the last time I saw Dorothy, I spoke with her on the telephone many times after that about my idea to create a calendar book to support new mothers in Grand Rapids, which she encouraged me to pursue. A couple of years later, thanks to Dorothy's guidance, I made a proposal to pediatric endocrinologist Dr. George Bacon, acting president of Butterworth Hospital, who quickly approved, and then handed me over to Fred Vandenberg, Chief Operating Officer at Butterworth Hospital. Fred also approved of such a book for new parents and handed me over to Priscilla Dakin, who guided me through the process of writing and publishing the 96-page, soft-cover *P.S. I Love You: Baby's 1st year Calendar Book* ©1997 by Butterworth Ventures, Inc. Completing it took a while to accomplish, including interviews with neonatologists, childlife specialists, nurses, other support staff, and a number of mothers and fathers themselves, nearly 50 individuals in all.

The table of contents lists the 24 chapters, each one describing why the early years of a child's life are the roots or foundation of a life that will produce "beautiful branches" as it evolves. What follows is from page 8 in *Your Baby's First Year, Your Baby's Personality or Temperament:*

> *Imagine that your baby is like a ball of clay. Clay is soft and easily formed just as some things about your baby can be shaped and molded by your words and actions. Thinking about this helps you to remember that your baby learns through her experiences with you and others. Now imagine that inside this clay is a small, hard ball that can never be shaped or changed. This ball is*

like your baby's personality or temperament, the part of her that makes her different from anyone else. You are not likely to change this inner personality much, nor do you want to. Your baby is who she is. That's what makes her special. Each baby is different from all others. Some babies are active, others are quiet, and some are in between. Pay attention to your baby's messages to you by the way she acts so you know when to add a little excitement and when to calm your baby down. Your baby's personality or temperament is her own. Value her for who she is. She will grow to value herself. She will also appreciate you, for allowing her to be who she is meant to be.

Shortly after it was published, thanks to Barbara Ivens of the Gerber Products Company, a generous grant from Gerber Products made it possible for DeVos Children's Hospital to publish thousands of complementary copies of the book to be given to new mothers delivering babies at Butterworth.

Several years after the book was published and handed out to new parents, I received a call from the Salvation Army in Grand Rapids. They asked me to come to their Grand Rapids location to meet a mother who was homeless and wanted to thank me for her copy of *P.S. I Love You*. Of course, I felt honored and humbled as I drove to the interview trying to imagine what this young mother would be like. She was waiting for me when I walked in the front door. Smiling shyly, she greeted me while holding her year-old baby daughter in one arm, and extending to me her copy of *P.S. I Love You* with the other. We sat down as she proudly showed me every page she filled out, from page 12 to page 63, one each for 52 weeks, with a few details for each day of the week—what her daughter ate, how she slept, where they were living at the time, who helped them, and the day her daughter laughed out loud for the first time. The three of us sat for over an hour as I listened to her tell about her life, her challenges and joys, with her main joy being a mother to her daughter. This was in 1998, nearly 25 years ago.

Every time I drive by the Salvation Army on Fulton Street, I think of that young mother and her daughter, how and where they are now. What would our world be like today if every baby born was loved and welcomed as that homeless mother welcomed and loved her baby?

As Sandra Day O'Connor[7] said, "We don't accomplish anything in this world alone. Whatever happens is the result of the whole tapestry of one's life and how all the weavings of individual threads can create something beautiful and lasting."

Once all the copies of *P.S. I Love You* were distributed, no more were published or distributed. Other programs and resources developed and evolved over time to incorporate the teachings and support the book provided at a time it was needed. More neonatologists, pediatric specialists and support staff joined the team at Helen DeVos Children's Hospital giving more and more newborns a better start in life.

Looking back on this special time in my life, in addition to the mother and her baby girl I think about often, I also remember fondly everyone who helped make the *P.S. I Love You* calendar book a reality for so many new mothers and fathers. I am also grateful to have known and worked with all of those dedicated and caring individuals who made the book possible.

---

[7] O'Conner was the first female associate justice of the Supreme Court of the United States from 1981 to 2006.

Chapter 16: Children Are Our Future

Cherishing children is the mark of a civilized society.
—Joan Ganz Cooney

The morning sky over Grand Rapids, Michigan, was a bright and cloudless blue on Monday, June 3, 1991, a perfect day for an outdoor event. Andy and I stood on a parking lot adjacent to Butterworth Hospital with nearly 200 other invited guests, waiting for the 10 a.m. groundbreaking ceremony to begin for a new women and children's health center.

The 11-story, $48 million tower would be named The Helen DeVos Women and Children's Center in honor of Helen DeVos as a result of a generous gift from her husband Richard. The gift would support pediatric programming and the new home for all of Butterworth's pediatric and women's health services.

Following remarks by several other speakers, Mrs. DeVos, a Grand Rapids native, former schoolteacher, community volunteer and mother of four grown children, stepped to the podium on the awning-covered dais. A slim, attractive woman in her mid-60s, she spoke quietly, yet distinctly and passionately about the importance of having specialized health care for children close to home.

"Butterworth Hospital has been very important in our family's life," she said, pausing to smile warmly at the large gathering of guests standing before her. "Four of our six grandchildren were born at Butterworth and our oldest grandchild spent time in Butterworth's neonatal intensive care unit.

"Because we know the value of having lifesaving care available close to home when a child is ill or injured, we feel very blessed to live in a community where all of you, as well, want this level of care available for children and families. After all, children are our future."

As a cluster of white doves was released into the sky at the conclusion of Mrs. DeVos's remarks, I sensed something great would evolve on that very site. It was as if those gentle birds were telling us the sky's the limit for what can be accomplished as a community that truly cares about its youngest and most vulnerable citizens.

Over the next 20 years as a free-lance writer for the Butterworth Foundation and later the Spectrum Health and Helen DeVos Children's Hospital Foundation, I would witness firsthand the amazing growth and development of this young institution, largely through the collective efforts of numerous individuals, the commitment of the Spectrum Health System in providing the best possible care for children, and the generous philanthropic and volunteer support not only from the DeVos family, but also from many others throughout the entire West Michigan community and beyond.

What touched me so profoundly, however, was meeting with so many dedicated care providers who told stories about why they had committed their careers and their very lives to the health and well-being for all children, often with great sacrifice to themselves and their own families. They told about sitting with the children themselves, and at times with the children's parents, listening as they told their stories, too, in their own words and in their own way, about the care they received at Helen DeVos Children's Hospital.

Chapter 17: Journaling for Joy

Happiness is temporary; joy is everlasting.
—Unknown

Once Andy and I were settled in Grand Rapids, I began looking forward to spending more fun and happy times with our kids. Eager to have them visit us in our new home, we also wanted our parents, siblings and other family members and friends to come to our place and celebrate holidays and birthdays together with us.

With everyone's busy lives, including ours, this wasn't as easy to arrange as I had hoped. Here we were, home alone at Christmas for the third time since we returned from Saudi Arabia and I wasn't happy. Instead, I was disappointed none of our kids came to spend any holiday time with us. This was before cell phones, so arranging visits via telephone calls back and forth on home phones shared with other family members was awkward. While I understood that we had been away for two years while they had established holiday routines with their other parents, grandparents, family and friends, I still missed seeing them as often as the others did.

By the afternoon of New Year's Day in 1994, I went from feeling sad, to feeling jealous and even angry. I imagined myself as both a motherless child and a childless mother since my mother had died 10 months earlier. I couldn't even call and talk with her on the phone as I did every week before she died. I also still missed my dad who died in 1987 of Alzheimer's disease after five years in a nursing home. My heart was heavy with self-pity and confusion. As much as Andy and I loved each other and our new lives in Grand Rapids, I couldn't help wondering what we had done to deserve spending holidays alone, especially at Christmas.

I told Andy I needed to be alone for a while, went into my office, closed the door, and picked up the journal I had written in only a few times in the three years since we'd been back. Although I quit writing in it as regularly as before, I picked up my pen and began filling page after page with thoughts, feelings and groundless fears about the future. How long I was there, I don't remember, but I will never forget what happened once I stopped writing—free of the emotional burdens I had been carrying for far too long, my head and heart felt lighter even though my hand was tired. Closing my journal, I put it away in a desk drawer, and didn't return to it until several days later.

After reading what I had written earlier, I felt I had become best friends with my "other self," the "pitiful Pam" who spilled out all the painful memories and emotions she had carried too long. With no tears or sadness, I felt compassion for myself and knew I had a choice: I could continue to act and feel like a victim, or together Andy and I could continue to create a life together while creating lives for ourselves, Andy as a doctor, me as a writer. I felt pure joy, and a renewed sense of gratitude about my ability to have a life with purpose and meaning beyond being a wife and mother. Happiness for me, I realized, had mostly depended on circumstances. Joy, I discovered on that Christmas, is a deeper sense of contentment I could feel even if things didn't turn out as I had wanted.

Having had the opportunity in Saudi Arabia to meet and get to know people from so many different cultures around the world and be able to write stories about them, was a gift from Andy who encouraged me to apply for the writing position at King Fahad National Guard Hospital. Once we came back home, I realized I could pursue a career as a freelance writer while being a loving and caring mother to my two nearly grown sons who didn't need me as they did when they were younger. I could also be a "second mother' to my nearly grown son and daughter by marriage who had a mother of their own they loved and wanted to spend time with, too.

I also began to realize that even though my parents were gone physically, they are still with me spiritually. Today, I feel their presence more than ever before, advising and encouraging me every day to follow my dreams—to be my own best friend and a writer of stories.

Chapter 18: The Power of Words

Put it before them briefly so they will read it, clearly so they will appreciate it, picturesquely so they will remember it, and, above all, accurately so they will be guided by its light.
—Joseph Pulitzer

Soon after I began writing articles for Butterworth Hospital's donor newsletter, I received a phone call from the president's secretary telling me he wanted me to write him a 'potent' speech. I didn't tell her I had never written a speech before. To make matters worse, I wasn't sure what he meant by 'potent'. Speech writing, I would soon learn, requires at least one in-depth interview, perhaps even two before putting words on paper. I hardly knew the man and he didn't know me, so before I could shape or "polish" his thoughts and intentions, I had to talk one-on-one with him to find out what he wanted to say before writing such an important speech. We arranged a time and date for our first interview, only a week away and only two weeks before he had to deliver his important speech. Plus, he wanted a first draft on his desk two days after our interview.

After she and I hung up, I pondered my options. Should I call her back and tell her I had never written a speech before and preferred to pass the job on to someone more qualified? Or should I keep our meeting for the first interview and give it a try?

Instead, I called a friend who listened as I described my dilemma. She suggested I try meditation and yoga instead of turning down an opportunity to do something new. She said if I relax and calm my mind, body and spirit, the words will come. She said worrying tightens us up and closes off our ability to be creative. When we worry, she said, we block the flow of positive energy—our birthright.

This was back in the early 1990s, so I went out and bought a few DVD tapes on yoga and meditation. I also subscribed to *Tricycle Magazine*[8] that described Buddhism as a philosophy, and/or a set of beliefs and practices based on the teachings of Siddhartha Gautama after

---

[8] www.tricycle.org

he attained enlightenment more than 2,600 years ago. I read, loved and still own and refer to Jack Kornfield's classic, *A Path With Heart*, that describes why and how he became a follower of Buddha, and how and why wisdom and compassion are the two most important spiritual gifts: wisdom being able to see things as they really are and compassion as knowing we are all One .

I came to realize that when I clung too tightly to something I wanted, or forcefully pushed away something I didn't want, I shut down and dried up my creative "juices." Another dear friend, my mentor Sister Sue Tracy, described fear as "false evidence appearing real" which was stopping me from living my dream. Doing yoga and attempting to meditate as often as I could made a difference. I began to see myself as a conduit rather than a creator of "potent" speeches and stories. I learned to open up my heart, mind and spirit before putting words on paper. I learned to leave time to reread and rewrite, and let it "sit" before I turned something in as a first draft.

Throughout my writing career, I'm come to see all of us as conduits of God's love, the energy of the Holy Spirit, the breath of life that gets me up in the morning, keeps me going during the day and comforts me when I go to sleep at night. Also, I never felt less a Christian for learning from and respecting Buddha's teachings. Knowing Buddha's story and how and why he went from being a privileged prince to a pitiful pauper and how he then "awakened" and moved to the Middle Way, neither privileged nor pitiful, inspired me to see myself similarly. As the middle daughter of a middle-class family born in the middle of WWII, I began to feel a new sense of freedom to be who I was—in the middle all the way —seeing life as both/and rather than either/or.

As it turned out, the speech I ended up writing for the hospital president was the first of many speeches I wrote not only for him but also for other hospital staff including major donors. I recorded all my interviews and transcribed them myself. Later, I gave all my recordings and transcriptions back to the hospital archivist. I never put words in anyone's mouth they didn't say themselves and feel passionate about.

Perhaps I used different words to clarify, but always with the same message they wanted to impart in as few words as possible.

Imagining myself as a "middle-of-the-way" conduit, all I did was come into the present moment with an open heart and mind while I listened to their stories. When writing the first draft of their speech, I tried to follow Pulitzer's advice about keeping it brief, bright and inspiring, while remembering Morton Blackwell's sage advice, "The mind can only absorb what the seat can endure."

Chapter 19: Through the Eyes of A Child

*When I told several private practice pediatricians
what I had been warned about, they laughed.*
James B. Fahner, M.D.

While I don't remember her name, how old she was, or the story I wrote about her older brother's successful treatment for cancer almost 30 years ago, I'll never forget what she said to me at the end of the interview. In just four words, this little girl taught me how profoundly one family member's illness can impact the lives of all family members.

My assignment that day was to meet with a young boy whose cancer was now in remission. The boy, no older than eight or nine, met me at Butterworth Hospital one afternoon with his parents and only sibling, a little girl, perhaps three or four, who played quietly with her doll in the corner of the room during the entire interview.

Initially, I questioned the parents about when they first heard about Butterworth Hospital's new program for pediatric cancer patients, and how and when they decided to make an appointment with Dr. James B. Fahner. In 1988, Dr. Fahner was a Fellow in pediatric oncology at the University of Michigan in Ann Arbor when he was recruited to come to Butterworth in 1989 to build the hospital's first pediatric hematology/ oncology program from the ground up.

The mother and father took turns expressing their gratitude for the excellent care their son had received and how thankful they were he was now in remission. They spoke about how difficult the early days and months of his illness were, when they weren't sure where to turn for care to save their son's life. Their personal situation was such that regular trips out of town for their son's cancer treatment would cause additional hardship for the entire family.

Next, I asked the boy how he felt about Dr. Fahner and his support staff team. The boy went on and on about how they not only helped him overcome his fears, they also caused him to look forward to appointments because he always had fun with a surprise gift they gave him to play with and keep that made him feel better.

After about 45 minutes, it was time to bring the interview to a close. I thanked the parents and their son for meeting with me and sharing their heartwarming story.

Just then, I felt a tap on my right knee. It was the little girl, holding her doll and looking up at me with a bit of sadness in her eyes after playing alone quietly in the corner of the room the entire time.

"I'm the little sister," she said shyly, hugging her doll even tighter as she turned and walked back toward her parents.

Of course, I thought, when a child is treated for a life-threatening disease such as cancer, the entire family is affected, not just the patient. This boy's little sister was part of the story, too, although I hadn't even asked the parents her name, and how her brother's illness had affected her. At the time, treatment for pediatric cancer was focused on the child, the one whose future depended on lifesaving care.

Looking back on those early days, Dr. Fahner said when he accepted the position at Butterworth in 1989, he was told he wouldn't be busy enough as a full-time employee of the hospital. Instead, he should join one of the private pediatric practices in town to fill his time.

"When I told several private practice pediatricians what I had been warned about, they laughed," he said. "As it turned out, I came to Butterworth Hospital for 438 straight days to see patients as the first and only pediatric hematologist/oncologist in West Michigan, until another pediatric hematologist/oncologist joined our team in 1991."

Today, Dr. Fahner is endowed division chief for the Ethie Haworth Children's Cancer Center at Helen DeVos Children's Hospital, thanks to a significant gift from the Haworth family in gratitude to Dr. Fahner and his team for curing their grandson of pediatric cancer.

Dr. Jim, known for his humility as he is for his incredible intellect, intelligence, leadership and character, said, "Personally, I couldn't be more proud and thrilled. But it's not about me. It's about the program and the positive impact we as a team have been able to create here that has and will continue to save the lives of so many children here in West Michigan and throughout our nation and world."

Chapter 20: Nick's Treasure Box

*Walk each day in childlike faith, with your hand
clasped in the hand of your Master.*
—White Eagle

Four-year-old Nick was the first pediatric patient at Butterworth Hospital
to undergo a bone marrow transplant. Nick was diagnosed with leukemia
at age two, received chemotherapy and went into remission for two
years. His cancer returned when he was four.

My first and only visit with Nick was when he was recovering from
his bone marrow transplant. I am thinking of both Nick and his mother as
I write this, wondering how she's doing today some 20 years later. She
was a wonderful mother to Nick, loving and supporting him throughout
his brief lifetime. Because of her, and Dr. Fahner and his team, Nick's
story is today an example for all of us on how to live each day to the
fullest even when life is cut short. Thus, I want to share what I learned
from Nick, and his mother, about the importance of living each day with
gratitude, humility, joy, humor and forgiveness of self and others.

Those of us who are growing older and reflecting on our earlier lives
can learn from this little boy who knew how to savor each day, regardless
of circumstances. This, to me, is Nick's most enduring legacy.

NICK's TREASURE BOX

A treasure box is symbolic of the unique treasure that lies within
each and every one of us. It's an outward sign of an inward essence, the
essence of who you are at the very core of your being and what your life
has meant to you and to those who know and love you.

Nick was a little boy who lived from a happy place deep inside
himself that felt like warm sunshine even on a dark day. He had a sparkle
about him that could overcome any feelings of doubt and fear, no matter
the circumstances. Even when he wasn't feeling well, he would often
break out in a smile when playing with a special toy, or when somebody
he knew walked into his hospital room.

Nick loved to explore his world when he was home between treatments. He didn't worry about the past; he didn't care about the future. He lived for the present moment, and had a zest for living that filled him with enthusiasm for even the most ordinary experiences.

Nick never went looking for treasures, they seemed to find him. Nick's imagination enabled him to celebrate all of life's special moments, even on a rainy day. For Nick, every day was a fresh canvas on which he created wonder-filled experiences. His enthusiasm combined with his innate curiosity and creativity colored his days, and ours, with wonder and beauty.

His mother said she sensed Nick knew he was dying, but he never let on because he didn't want his family to worry about him.

"In spite of his leukemia, Nick loved every day of his life. He was a free spirit who knew who he was," she said.

"Nick was our hero because a hero shows up in life, even when it's scary. He never wished he could be someone else and he never complained about being sick. He lived with hope and with the full knowledge that death may be hastened by his leukemia. From the moment we knew he had cancer, he was a survivor. Being a survivor is about living with the hope that life will continue, and that if and when death comes, it is neither a defeat nor a failure. Nick knew, intuitively, he had a purpose to fulfill in his lifetime. It was as if he knew he had something to accomplish that no one could accomplish for him."

His mother told me Nick collected all kinds of things such as key chains and erasers, Hot Wheels cars and bugs. He loved hearts of all shapes and sizes, and whether they were stones or leaves or scraps of paper, they were his treasures he kept in his big, plastic bin he called his Treasure Box.

"Nick's treasures provided comfort from the pain and isolation, the frustrations of not being able to do what other kids did to have fun," she said. "Nick made his own fun by savoring the moment and then keeping something from that moment to remember forever."

Chapter 21: Love Without Boundaries

"The question, 'Why do children suffer?' has no answer, unless it's simply, 'To break our hearts.' Once our hearts get broken, they never fully heal. They always ache. But perhaps a broken heart is a more loving instrument. Perhaps only after our hearts have cracked wide open, have finally and totally unclenched, can we know love without boundaries.
—Fred J. Epstein, M.D.

Stephen Duren's heart had been broken before, but this time it cracked wide open.

It was a dark and bitterly cold late evening in January of 1992, when he and Adelle's mother were told by a surgeon at Blodgett Memorial Medical Center that their 10-year-old daughter Adelle had an inoperable, malignant brain tumor. Adelle had undergone a similar surgery at Blodgett earlier but the findings were much more positive then. Now, three years later, even with the support of chemotherapy, the Durens were told their daughter would live only four to six months.

"When you're hit with the potential death of your child," said Mr. Duren, well known West Michigan artist, "you're so emotionally devastated that you can almost no longer think for yourself. Whatever hand reaches out to you and points, then that's the direction you go."

Adelle's story is remarkable because of how both she and her parents responded to this news. "When your child is gravely ill, you feel so helpless," Stephen Duren said. "When you're given the prognosis that she's going to die and there's nothing you can do, there's nothing you can do but accept it. One part of me had to accept her death but this other part of me refused to accept it. When a friend sent us an article out of *Ladies Home Journal* magazine featuring Dr. Epstein, an internationally renowned pediatric neurosurgeon, that was all I needed.

"All the doctors I called before I learned about Dr. Epstein told me they could help Adelle but only to extend her life," said Mr. Duren. "None of them said they could save her life, that is until I called Dr. Epstein's office in New York."

Up to this point, Stephen Duren had been working as hard as he could as a young, unknown artist to pay the medical bills stacking up since Adelle's headaches and other symptoms began in 1987. When he told Dr. Epstein the family had zero money, Dr. Epstein told the Durens to bring her anyway. They'd worry about that later.

"The Butterworth Pediatric Hematology/Oncology program headed by Dr. Jim Fahner came to our rescue by connecting us with two social workers who said they could help with the finances. I remember it hit me like a ton of bricks when we realized that with their help we were actually going to make this work," said Mr. Duren.

After filling out countless forms and undergoing numerous interviews to get funding, Adelle and her parents were on their way to New York City for Adelle's third, and final brain surgery. But this time, she would be under the care of the only surgeon in the world who would attempt to remove a tumor from the brain stem. All this within weeks of her second surgery that was thought to be her last.

"My third surgery was especially hard on my nerves," said Adelle. "It seemed at every turn the hospital staff wanted to tear me away from my parents. They felt my parents were in the way. I was incredibly insecure and vulnerable. In Grand Rapids, my parents were with me for each surgery until I was asleep.

"I didn't like anything about New York City except Dr. Epstein. I was terribly homesick and wanted to get out of the city and back home. The New York University Medical Center was not user friendly, but Dr. Epstein sure was. He made me feel protected. He even told me I could call him Fred," she said.

After surgically removing Adelle's tumor successfully at New York University Hospital, Dr. Epstein agreed to be the keynote speaker at the first annual Helen DeVos Lectureship at the Amway Grand Plaza Hotel on August 18, 1993, 13 days before the new Helen DeVos Women and Children's Center opened.

The event was to honor Helen DeVos and the extraordinary contributions she and her family made to the West Michigan community. Seated at the head table the evening of the event with Dr. Epstein and

Rich and Helen DeVos were Dr. Jim and Gail Fahner who overheard a conversation between Dr. Epstein and Rich DeVos.

"Now just wait," said Dr. Epstein to Mr. DeVos, "with this state-of-the-art facility, you will attract the best and brightest young physicians, nurses and staff." Mr. DeVos waved his hand toward the Fahners and across the crowded room. "Look around these tables, doctor," Mr. DeVos said without missing a beat. "Many of them are already here."

Dr. Epstein knew what it was to be a child who suffered. Diagnosed in his early years with profound learning disabilities, he was rejected from several medical schools before being accepted and eventually graduating from New York University and New York Medical College. Dr. Epstein was later credited with pioneering neurological techniques to successfully treat children threatened by brain and spinal-cord tumors, something that had never been attempted before.

Today, Stephen Duren is a proud and grateful father and grandfather. When I emailed him for permission to share Adelle's story in my book, he quickly responded. "Thirty-four years later, the drama that Adelle experienced, beginning at age seven, is never far from my thoughts. Hard to believe she is now 41 years old, happily married and with a beautiful daughter of her own."

So many aspects of this story continue to touch my heart, after being a writer and a forever champion for Helen DeVos Children's Hospital in my retirement years. First that Adelle's life was saved by her father's persistent refusal to give up. Also, Dr. Epstein's childhood experience gave him the compassion and courage to pursue a career that saved many lives in addition to Adelle's, all a result of his refusal to give up, too. And finally, it's Dr. Epstein's quote about how to answer the question, "Why do children suffer," that tugs at my heart every time I read it, and I trust at every other person's heart who also reads it. I assume he was asked such a question many times during his career. Dr. Epstein's response, "Perhaps only after our hearts have cracked wide open, have finally and totally unclenched, can we truly know love without boundaries," is a message our world needs to hear more often today.

Sadly, Dr. Epstein died in 2006 of melanoma at age 68, but his legacy lives on in the lives of those whose lives he saved, including Adelle's. He also wrote two books for general readers, *Gifts of Time*, published in 1993, and *If I Get to Five*, published in 2003. Also a prolific writer of numerous articles for professional publications, Dr. Epstein was known primarily for his skill as a neurosurgeon and his compassion and respect for children.

When Dr. Epstein came to Grand Rapids thirty years ago for the Helen DeVos Lectureship event, Adelle was excited to see him again.

"The first thing out of my mouth when I saw him was, 'Look, Fred, my hair is growing long again and I made this skirt all by myself,'" she said. "He smiled at me, knelt down, and gave me a hug. Although I never remembered thanking him for fixing my brain, I am sure he knew I meant 'thank you'."

Chapter 22: Friends Are Like Angels

Friends are like angels without any wings,
blessing our lives with more precious things.
—Martin J. Besteman

The first time I met Martin Besteman, he was a proud grandfather hosting a gathering of friends to celebrate a book I wrote in 2011, the year I officially retired as a free-lance writer for Helen DeVos Children's Hospital. Without Martin's granddaughter, Tara, the book, titled *Through the Eyes of a Child,* would never have been published in such a timely way. Tara, as a member of the Helen DeVos Children's Hospital Foundation staff, ably and enthusiastically partnered with me throughout the final phase of approvals and publishing that same year.

This special occasion was Martin's way to express his pride and joy for Tara. The book itself was my gift to the hospital for the privilege of being a writer of stories about children and families whose lives were saved and changed there. All 3,000 copies of the book were eventually sold or given away, with all profits going to programs and services at Helen DeVos Children's Hospital that rely on philanthropy.

At the time, Martin was 89 years young, although he appeared much younger when he greeted my husband and me at the retirement facility where he and Martha, his wife of 68 years, lived. Along with Tara, Martin and Martha, Andy and I soon sat down for a delicious lunch along with perhaps a dozen or more guests, family and friends of Martin's.

Unbeknownst to me, Martin had purchased a generous number of books from the hospital gift shop and gave them to those who were there that day. Others who couldn't attend the luncheon wrote letters. What follows are a few comments in the file of letters Martin passed on to me.

One fellow wrote: "I was especially impacted by the fact that there were so many people who did so many good things to help children."

Another wrote: "People love to read stories of hope, stories of success, and about people they know and admire, like Rich DeVos and his family."

In another handwritten letter, a friend said, "I was so impressed with the dedication and perseverance of the doctors who were so convinced that this hospital was going to happen! I remember the competition between the two hospitals, Butterworth and Blodgett to create Spectrum Health. The merger accomplished so much! So many have worked hard and given so much, in different ways, to bring about this wonderful regional children's hospital. The book was a real awakening!"

Sister Sue Tracy, a chaplain at Helen DeVos Children's Hospital, wrote: "This book captures the impacting story of multiple generous people who pooled funds time and time again to help build the $286 million treasure we now have in the heart of downtown Grand Rapids." She went on to include quotes from others who were interviewed: "Quality attracts quality and quality seeks out quality . . . children are not just little adults, they have very special needs medically . . . history is important but the future is where we're going . . . there is nothing we cannot achieve, once we set our minds to it."

One of the most touching responses was a handwritten letter from a woman who wrote about a child I will call Brenda, born in the early 1980s. She wrote, "Brenda spent more time in the hospital than at home her first year of life. Brenda's next seven years were spent looking for a diagnosis for her illness. We traveled back and forth to Ann Arbor and Mayo Clinic for many years because there were not enough specialists in the 1980s.

"By 1991, nine years after her birth, Dr. Stephen Barbour diagnosed Brenda with a blood disorder and she came under the care of Dr. James Fahner, a wonderful caring doctor. Brenda had a syndrome that only two children in the state had at that time. After 1991, we never had to leave the city to find treatment."

In the file Martin handed to me as we were saying good-bye after the luncheon, was the invitation he sent to numerous friends to tell them about the book and why they should read it. He included two quotes, the first one appears at the top of the previous page. The second one is something we all need to remember: "You're only as pretty as the smile on your face and the thoughts that fill your heart."

Wise words for all ages from a man who lived to be 92, and described in his obituary as, " . . . a loving husband, dad, grandpa, and great grandpa, who had a great sense of humor."

Martin's wisdom and humor are validated by Irish poet, William Butler Yeats, in what is one of my all-time favorite poems, especially now as I strive to grow older without growing old. This sage advice was modeled to me by Martin and so many others I write about in this my collection of stories for you, dear reader, along with a selection of references in the Appendix to help you write your own stories.

A Dialogue of Self and Soul

I am content to follow to its source
Every event in action or in thought;
Measure the lot; forgive myself the lot!
When such as I cast out remorse
So great a sweetness flows into the breast
We must laugh and we must sing,
We are blest by everything,
Everything we look upon is blest.

—William Butler Yeats

Chapter 23: Diane Z's Best Advice Ever

After a while you learn that you really can endure,
that you really are strong, and you really do have worth.
And you learn and learn, with every good-bye you learn.
—Jorge Luis Borges

After Andy and I got settled in Grand Rapids, Michigan, one of my first assignments as a free-lance writer for Butterworth Hospital was to interview Diane Zarafonetis.

Diane Z, as she was affectionately known by her many fans and friends, had an unforgettable flair for making others feel important. Being new in town and somewhat unsure of myself, I came to regard Diane as my big sister, even though she was three years younger.

Young, attractive, happily married with two children, Diane had a loving family, a home, many friends—and breast cancer. When I first met her, Diane was completely bald from chemotherapy—and beautiful. Refusing to wear a wig, she was determined not to hide the fact she had cancer, but to stand tall in her determination to beat it. People were drawn to her because she wasn't afraid to talk about cancer without making it the center of attention.

At age 38, when she underwent a double mastectomy at Butterworth Hospital, Diane told me when she came out of surgery in acute physical and emotional pain, the nurse said to her, "I know how you feel."

For a split second, Diane said she felt less alone in her loss and suffering, assuming her nurse knew exactly how she was feeling.

"Did you have a double mastectomy, too?" Diane asked.

"No, but I know how you feel," the nurse answered.

Diane let the nurse know in no uncertain terms to never tell a patient she knows how they feel unless she's undergone the same experience.

Diane recovered from her surgery with a mission. She wanted to form a support group for other women with breast cancer, all recently diagnosed, recovering or recovered from breast cancer, who could share their stories with others going through similar experiences. With mutual support and wholehearted sisterhood, they could support each other, cry with each other, laugh with each other, and celebrate life with each other, one day at a time.

This was back in the early 1980s when it was common for people to refer to cancer as "The Big C." Diane said when she asked her oncologist for other patients of his with breast cancer, he refused. Unintimidated, Diane's response was, "People in Grand Rapids won't even say the word 'breast' unless they're ordering chicken."

With humor and unstoppable creativity Diane persevered with passion and persistence. In 1988, *Expressions*, the first support group in West Michigan for women with breast cancer, was born. Diane died in early the evening of May 21, 1997, at age 50, but not without a fight. Today, she would be 76, and just as beautiful and full of life as she was in her prime.

A while ago, I came across remarks I made at a gathering of cancer survivors honoring Diane's life and legacy. I told the group gathered that Diane taught me it isn't what happens to you in life, it's how you respond to what happens. The messages I shared with them that day came from Diane herself, who always said, "Attitude is everything."

Eat Your Dessert First: Diane lived life with joy and gratitude rather than obligation and guilt. She always said, "If you don't love what you're doing and who you're doing it with, don't do it."

Live Life in a Wellness Mode Not an Illness Mode: Diane said her disease did not define her or how she lived her life. "Breast cancer is nobody's first choice, but it's not the end of the world, either," she said.

Own Your Illness; Own Your Recovery: Diane took responsibility for the quality of her day and her mood. This sense of ownership was very empowering for her and she inspired others to do the same.

Self-Love Doesn't Mean Selfish: Diane's main message to all women everywhere, not only women with breast cancer, was that denial of feelings can be self-destructive. "What you can't express, you can't heal," she said from her own experience, which inspired her to call the support group she founded *Expressions*.

Chapter 24: Six Books

Don't Get all your Information From One Source
—The Wall Street Journal

Nearly 50 years ago when I lived in Petoskey, my best friend Jan and I drove to her parents' home in Holland, Michigan, for a weekend visit. At the dinner table each night and at the breakfast table each morning, Jan's father read a few lines of scripture in the Bible, and a brief message-for-the-day from several other books.

I was so impressed and inspired by Jan's parents, their modest yet comfortable, well kept and cheerful home, the way they lovingly and respectfully treated each other and their five daughters and how they treated me, their guest, that their habit of reading spiritual messages every day became my habit, too. I could easily see that Jan's parents' faith was what gave them the will to live confidently in spite of challenges and hardships they overcame with love.

Shortly after returning home, I hosted a coffee for our women's group at First Presbyterian Church. One of our members read from a little pocket-sized, non-denominational, monthly magazine, *Daily Word,* published by Unity, and I was so inspired by its message that I've been a subscriber ever since. In 1989, *Daily Word* went with me to Saudi Arabia, as it goes with us every night we are away from home, whether for one night or two weeks or more. I am never without it.

In 1991, when Andy and I returned from Saudi Arabia, a friend I met after we settled in Grand Grand Rapids told me about *Guide for Spiritual Living,* the Science of Mind magazine published by Centers for Spiritual Living. The magazine's articles and messages appealed to me so much that we began subscribing to it, too.

Over the years, we've collected other inspirational books: *Today's Gift : Daily Meditations for Families* by the Hazelden Foundation, *Daily Reflections for Highly Effective People* by Stephen R. Covey, *Pocketful of Miracles* by Joan Borysenko, and *The Promise of a New Day: A Book of Daily Meditations* by the Hazelden Foundation.

Today, as we take turns every morning reading aloud from our six books, I often think of Jan's parents, Rich and Jean, both now deceased. Their example not only positively changed my life during the eight years I found myself single again, but also has continued to enhance the life Andy and I share together today.

While these books are familiar to us, many other books are just as inspiring, just as motivating, just as soul and spirit strengthening and enriching depending on one's faith tradition. Both of us read a variety of books, mostly non-fiction. While none of us can read them all, we can choose to read from a variety of sources which is better than reading from only one. We also have quotes that sustain us every day, words we can quickly see and repeat to ourselves through the day. Two quotes I have posted here in my office are: *Be Kind*, and *If you do little things well, you'll do big ones better.*

Some may be surprised to learn that Andy keeps a photograph of Joseph Stalin on his desk with a quote from *The Wall Street Journal*, *Don't get all your information from one source.* Anyone born in the 1940s and earlier knows Joseph Stalin was the Soviet leader of the Russian army. It was Stalin who forced Andy and his parents, grandmother and brother to flee their home in Latvia with only the clothes on their backs in 1944.

While Andy's experience growing up was very different from mine, what wasn't different was the care and nurturing he received from both his parents who did all they could to raise their family with the same values and virtues they were raised with during very difficult times. Although the cultures Andy and I grew up in were different, our parents were very much the same in how lived their faith by how they lived their lives each day.

This is why I remain confident that while our world may seem out of control at times, justice, prosperity and sustainability will come, perhaps not in my lifetime, but before it's too late. We *can* and *will* come together to find common ground by listening, learning, sharing, and synthesizing what we have learned from each other to create a better world for all through better communication, cooperation and collaboration.

Chapter 25: A Crisis of Consciousness

I believe the sustainability crisis can be described as a crisis generated by our lack of deep self-awareness.
—Chris Bache

In 1996, I attended my first Institute of Noetic Sciences (IONS) Annual Conference held in Palm Desert, CA, surrounded by the Santa Rosa Mountains. Early one morning, I walked alone to the main conference center for breakfast and found my way to the outdoor patio with my coffee and toast. Only one other early riser was seated at one of the tables enjoying the full view of the sun rising above the mountain peaks. When he asked if I wanted to join him, I said yes. When he introduced himself, I found myself shaking hands with none other than Edgar Mitchell, founder of the Institute of Noetic Sciences and retired United States Navy officer and aviator, test pilot, aeronautical engineer, ufologist (the study of UFOs), NASA astronaut and the sixth man to walk on the moon. As the Lunar Module Pilot of Apollo 14, Dr. Mitchell spent nine hours working on the lunar surface in the Fra Mauro Highlands region.

What I remember most about our pleasant conversation that morning was Dr. Mitchell's passion for reconnecting science and spirituality. My one-on-one conversation with an educated and experienced expert—a man who had walked on the moon and came back to Earth to tell about it —was life-changing for me. What he and I talked about validated my college experiences and confirmed what I had always suspected—that faith and science, split apart in the 17th and 18th centuries that emphasized reason and individualism over tradition, are complementary. Before that day, I had never shared my stories about my biology and astronomy professors with anyone else, but I did with Dr. Mitchell. He listened carefully as I described to him my own thoughts about perpetual patterns. To my enormous delight, he validated them.

Today, it is now an accepted fact, at least among the most evolved scientists and religious scholars, that science is "proving" what people of all the faith traditions, including indigenous peoples, have known since the beginning of time. We are not self-made. Rather, we are created by a

Higher Power that created the Universe. We ARE made of starstuff. We are all more alike than different. We are all interconnected, and we continue to evolve. Nothing is stationary, everything belongs. We all belong.

What's more, scientists are proving that plants, trees and shrubs—all growing things—also have intelligence and are interconnected with each other, as with all of us. All creation is far more amazing, far more miraculous than even we in the 21st century can imagine.

I love reflecting on these memories from my life that are still with me today. Writing them down keeps me energized and gives me a deeper awareness of who I am, why I am here, where I've come from, and where I am going when my life on Mother Earth is over.

As Harlow Shapley so clearly stated in his introduction to *View From a Distant Star*, humanity's future "will depend on how well s/he understands the requirements for survival and how willing s/he is to struggle for the peaceful creation of a viable world society." I added the s/he to Shapley's original "he" and substituted "humanity" for his original "mankind," because if we are to be successful in bringing lasting peace to Mother Earth, we must do this with both male and female energies and intelligences as an equal yet dynamic partnership.

Even us elders have an active role to play in this struggle for the peaceful creation of a viable world society. After all, we have children and grandchildren we love more than life itself. We want to pass the world onto them in better shape than we found it, not in worse shape. Thus, we must continue to live our best lives as conscious stewards of Mother Earth until we take our last breath. As Robert Frost said so well in his poem *Stopping by Woods on a Snowy Evening*, "I have promises to keep and miles to go before I sleep, and miles to go before I sleep," and this includes all of us still alive, regardless of age or circumstance.

Chapter 26: The Little Red Hen Revisited

It will never rain roses: when we want to have
more roses, we must plant more roses.
—George Eliot

Little Golden Books were among my favorite childhood books. Appearing on the market in 1942, *Little Golden Books* were the first high-quality books for children most parents could afford. Priced at just 25 cents and available where people shopped every day, they quickly gained popularity and were sold by the hundreds of thousands.

My all-time favorite is still *The Little Red Hen*, nearly seven decades later. In fact, *The Little Red Hen* first appeared in a Little Golden Book in 1943, the year I was born. To me, hers is a timeless message relevant yet today.

The Little Red Hen is a story about effective leadership and teamwork. The hen herself demonstrates how even a chicken can have agency over her own life while encouraging other animals in the barnyard to do the same. Her story begins when she asks the other animals to pitch in so she can make bread. She needs someone to help plant the wheat, harvest the wheat, grind the wheat to make flour and bake the bread. Instead, they holler, "I'm too tired," or "I'm not interested," or "I'm too busy," or simply, "Not I."

Thus, the Little Red Hen decides to make the bread herself. She plants the wheat, harvests and grinds the wheat, and forms the bread into loaves. When the loaves come out of the oven, all crusty and golden brown, their enticing scent fills the air with an aroma the animals can't resist. When the Little Red Hen asks, "Who will help me eat my bread?" one by one they answer affirmatively.

But the Little Red Hen surprises them all. "None of you were willing to help me plant the wheat, harvest the wheat, grind the wheat to make flour and help me bake my bread," she says firmly. "So none of you shall have any. I shall eat it all myself."

For many years, the original ending to this story left me with an uneasy feeling. I'd often thought about "tweaking" the end to impart a more positive message. From a spiritual sense, we are all born equal, born to love and be loved, born to create. Not all of us come into families that welcome us with love and a safe and secure home where parents teach life lessons by example, within a faith tradition that edifies the Golden Rule. I've always loved the verse from Luke 12:48 that says, "To whom much is given, much is expected in return."

Thus, in the revised version of *The Little Red Hen*, our heroine asks the farm animals to help her with the planting, the harvesting, the grinding and the baking, and tells them IF they wish to enjoy eating the bread after it's baked, they all must do their part to help. She begins by explaining the various steps necessary to produce a loaf of freshly baked bread. Next, she asks each animal what they would enjoy doing to share in the work and assist in the process.

The cow speaks up first. "I'd like to plant the seeds, and offer my manure to enrich the soil," she says with a mighty, "Moooo."

The horse says, "I'd like to help with the harvest by using my strength to pull the wagon."

The pig oinks happily and says, "I'd like to grind the wheat, slowly and evenly, around and around to grind it to a fine flour."

The cat, awakening from a nap, yawns and says, "I'd like to knead the dough by working it with my paws, up and down, up and down, until it's ready to rise and go into the oven."

"Wonderful," says the Little Red Hen, "then we shall have a feast when the bread is baked. We'll celebrate our team effort with each of us doing something we like to do and what we do best. Everyone can contribute something essential to the outcome."

With a happy cackle, she adds, "It just so happens I made a batch of homemade strawberry jam to spread on our freshly baked bread."

Can't you just see the farm animals sitting around the table celebrating with freshly baked bread and homemade strawberry jam? I can hear them all now making plans for a larger harvest next year of potatoes and beans, lettuce and cabbage, beets and broccoli so they can invite animals from the neighboring farms. None of them, of course, would suggest anything other than a vegetarian feast!

Chapter 27: A Girl With a Book

The most terrifying image for a terrorist.
—Malala Yousafzai

Following are excerpts from remarks I made in 2019 to members of PEO here in West Michigan, a U.S.-based international women's organization with a primary focus on providing educational opportunities for female students worldwide.

In 2014, a documentary, *The Uncondemned*[9], was released, telling the story of how four years after the Rwandan massacres took place, Jean-Paul Akayesu (Ah-kee-AY-soo), a former mayor, was convicted on nine counts of genocide and crimes against humanity, including rape and sexual violence. Dozens more convictions followed, among them the former Rwandan Prime Minister Jean Kambanda, who became the first head of a government ever to be convicted of genocide by rape by an international court.

I knew about this because Sara Darehshori, daughter of our good and longtime friends, served as co-counselor of the Rwandan War Tribunal at The Hague. Sara was able to convince the women who were raped to tell their stories. As a result of her persistence and respect for the truth, and the women's courage, rape was prosecuted as a war crime for the first time since officially made a crime in WWI.

On July 12, 2017 (two years ago) Malala Yousafzai made a speech to the U.N. General Assembly in NYC.

In her speech she said, "Today, I am focusing on women's rights and girls' education because they are suffering the most."

She also said, "I do not even hate the Taliban who shot me. Even if there is a gun in my hand and he stands in front of me, I would not shoot him. This is the compassion I have learned from Mohammad, Jesus, Buddha, Martin Luther King, and Mother Teresa."

At the close of her speech she said:

---

[9] *Available on YouTube*

"So let us wage a global struggle (notice she doesn't say "war") against illiteracy, poverty and terrorism and let us pick up our books and pens. They are our most powerful weapons. The most terrifying image for a terrorist is a girl with a book! One child, one teacher, one pen and one book can change the world. Education is the only solution. Education First."

An increasingly important message for us older women—and all older individuals regardless of gender—is to share our stories, share the wisdom we've learned through our own experiences, not to preach but to teach and pass on the virtues and values we've learned without passing on the pain, and to acknowledge that we're still learning, every single day of our lives.

Yes, things are changing and much of it for good reason and long overdue; however, the values of kindness and caring, responsibility and courage, perseverance and wisdom are timeless. How did I learn these things? Not from a book, but from my parents, teachers, grandparents, friends, and not always because they did it right. Many of them made mistakes, too, and either they realized it, and owned it, or the effects of their mistakes were felt for years afterward. I learned through my own mistakes, by not being conscious or aware of my own "shadow" which I am still learning about through the Enneagram and my own writing.

I've also learned the importance of forgiveness—of self and others. To me, this has been the biggest lesson of all and the hardest to learn. Not forgiving creates so many more problems. But forgiving too soon, before you've learned the lesson, can be harmful, too, especially to yourself.

Chapter 28: Mrs. Rau's Timeless Teaching

It's the little details that are vital.
Little things make big things happen.
—John Wooden

My first grade teacher was Mrs. Blodwyn Rau, an elegant, well dressed, older lady with grey hair who welcomed us students warmly by name everyday as we walked in the door of her classroom. I had never heard the name Blodwyn before, although we called her Mrs. Rau. Recently, I looked up the origin of the name Blodwyn and learned it's Welsh, meaning white flower, which describes Mrs. Rau perfectly.

Today, some 74 years later, I still think of Mrs. Rau when I use a restroom because of what she taught me when I was six years old. I also wonder how many other girls in our class still remember, too.

One day, Mrs. Rau instructed us girls to follow her in a straight line for a short walk down the hall to the girls' restroom. I assume our student teacher Miss Marjorie Willock was in charge of the boys who stayed behind. What I especially remember was what Mrs. Rau showed us to do with the paper towel after drying our hands. She demonstrated by washing her hands with soap, rising them well, reaching for one paper towel only, drying her hands thoroughly, then wading the towel up into a little ball before dropping it in the wastebasket.

She explained that washing our hands after using the restroom is sanitary and keeps us healthy. It also prevents towels from filling up the wastebasket too quickly and going all over the floor. Even in a private restroom, wash your hands with soap and water, dry them with whatever towel is available, return the towel folded wherever you found it, or, if paper, wad it up into a little ball and drop it in the wastebasket.

Why, I wonder, do I have trouble remembering where I left my keys or what day it is, when I vividly remember such seemingly insignificant events from so many years ago, although I do not consider them insignificant.

Albert Einstein, who considered himself agnostic, "a religious nonbeliever,"once said, "The most beautiful thing we can experience is the mysterious. Insight into the mystery of life, coupled though it be with fear, has also given rise to religion. To know what is impenetrable to us really exists, manifesting itself as the highest wisdom and the most radiant beauty, which our dull faculties can comprehend only in their most primitive forms—this knowledge, this feeling is at the center of true religiousness."

I agree, only what he describes as mystery, I describe as faith. But it's not the words themselves that count. It's the power in the meaning the words convey that affect how we live our lives, day by day.

Chapter 29: Love Is . . .

The opposite of a correct statement is a false statement. But the opposite of a profound truth may well be another profound truth.
—Niels Bohr

Love is a word of unlimited interpretation and meaning. I love my husband, I love our home, our kids, family, friends, books, dates and peanut butter, and my very life. All are different kinds of love. Some I can hug, some I enjoy being with, some I can hold in my hand; some I can eat; all I hold in my heart.

It's easy to love something that loves you back, or something that's going well. It's quite another to love something that's not going well, or someone who's "pushing your buttons" and something that disappoints, whether it's a pie you baked, a friend you thought was a friend, and a day that didn't turn out the way you wanted it to.

Defined by Merriam-Webster as a noun and a verb, love is a feeling, an emotion, and love is an action you take through hard work and sacrifice, a choice made not because it's in your best interest alone but because it's in the best interest of yourself and others, even a stranger. First responders give their lives to help others in danger without asking their religion, politics or ethnicity out of love for humanity. Soldiers give their lives for love of country and duty. To me, love is more of a verb than a noun. Giving to others gives our own lives purpose and meaning as long as we don't give ourselves away by feeling 'less than' others, for each life is a gift to our world and every life is precious.

Love is a choice—the ultimate paradox, changing and fluctuating all the time and yet unchangeable, immutable, eternal. Love is not either/or; love is both/and—the ability to hold two polarities in creative tension, as described by Sydney J. Harris in his pocket-sized classic, *The Authentic Person: Dealing With Dilemma*. As Harris says on pp. 40, "Adopting a middle-of-the-road position is usually just tepidity and timidity, but to grasp a paradox and to hold it in tension, requires courage and wisdom."

Some believe God's love for creation is the invisible force that created our world and Universe and holds them in perfect balance with all matter. Some scientists studying particle physics say the Higgs Boson particle, first sighted on December 13, 2011, holds the Universe together. My view is that love is both science and spirituality.

One of my favorite quotes by Pierre Teilhard de Chardin describes his vision of humanity's next great awakening and transformation and its significance in the history and evolution of humanity: "The day will come when, after harnessing space, the winds, the tides, and gravitation, we shall harness for God the energies of love. And, on that day, for the second time in the history of the world, we shall have discovered fire."

Rather than being on a hierarchy of more or less value, I see love as concentric circles with a common center. When love is learned early in life, the capacity to love others who are different, to love ourselves even when we fail and disappoint, and the ultimate love—the ability to love and forgive our enemies—increases exponentially as one matures.

While love can be learned at any age, seeds of love are best planted within a baby from the moment of conception. Later, how baby is welcomed into the world by its parents and other family members is how that baby, in time, will learn to love others. We humans don't come into the world knowing how to love. We learn to love by being loved first.

Some define love as a feeling, an emotion, a sense of wholeness, security and comfort. To me, love is mostly about how I choose to spend my time, talents and treasure, how to act day in and day out. Love is how I choose to behave, how I choose to think, to speak, to treat others, to care for myself, to care for Andy's and my belongings, the belongings of others, our neighbors and our neighborhood.

Love is what gets me out of bed each morning as I begin a new day. Love is what I am passionate about and how I spend money, time and energy. Love is how we give back to our communities, how we treat strangers, how we work to preserve our environment, how we treat our families, friends, everything in our lives, including how we love and treat ourselves. Love to me is divine energy we are all made of and what gives us the ability to breathe, make choices, participate freely in life, experience life in all its fullness, and to love all of God's creation—past, present and future—as much as we love ourselves.

Chapter 30: Forgiveness

To forgive is one of the greatest gifts
you can give yourself. Forgive everybody.
–Maya Angelou

Whenever someone asks me what I've been doing lately, I say, "Downsizing and simplifying." Recently, I made great progress clearing out our storage room. I read through and recycled a stack of three-ring notebooks of my daily reflections the past 20 years. I also re-read a diary I've had since I was 10. My ramblings as a ten-year-old were mostly about school and Girl Scouts, our various pets, weekend fun and creative at-home projects. My later writings chronicled the ups and downs of family life and other relationship issues including my complaints of menopause and coming to grips with the reality of growing older. Rereading through these diaries, I noticed my mood swings from depressed to delighted, grateful for my faith in God, my relationship with Andy, my sons and grandkids, our families and siblings, close friends and work colleagues. I also noticed I would often close with renewed commitment to being more loving, more understanding, more aware of my own faults and weaknesses, and mostly more forgiving.

One of the stories from my earlier years that came to mind as I sifted through all these memories took place in the fall of my sophomore year at Ohio State. I was living at home although I joined a sorority where many of my sorority sisters smoked. I took up smoking hoping it would make me appear "cool" and sophisticated. Those were the days before cigarette smoking was known to cause lung cancer and other serious health problems. Besides, I only smoked socially, at the sorority house or with my friends who smoked, but never, ever at home or in front of anyone who would tell my parents.

It was a beautiful fall day in 1962, when I borrowed Daddy's new Buick to drive over to my aunt and uncle's home a few miles east of Worthington. Their restored 19th century home was on the Worthington Historical Society's Tour of Homes and I was a volunteer hostess. Driving Daddy's fancy new car gave me a sense of pride and privilege along with a chance to light up a Winston cigarette without anyone being the wiser. Unknowingly to me, when I threw the cigarette out the front window, it came in through the open back window and landed in the backseat of Daddy's car. A number of cars were already parked in the driveway by the time I pulled onto their property. I had been inside for only 20 minutes or so when someone shouted from the backyard, "Call the fire department, quick! A car's on fire out here!"

By the time firefighters arrived and put out the flames, Daddy's new car was ruined. I honestly don't remember how I got home, whether Aunt Charlotte or someone else brought me, but what I vividly remember is coming in the front door and immediately going upstairs to my bedroom. I closed my bedroom door and sat on my bed in the dark wondering what I could possibly do to make up for what I had done. Daddy knew of my bad habit, never scolded me for it, although he reminded me now and then that it wasn't a healthy thing to do. He smoked cigars, or rather chewed them. Mother was a social smoker, never at home or in front of me and my sisters. Now that Daddy's new car was out of commission for a while, I fully expected him to be furious, take away my driving privileges and ground me. When he finally knocked on my door and asked if he could come in, he sat down, put his arm around me and said firmly and sympathetically, "You won't do that ever again, will you, Pammy?"

"No, Daddy, I won't," I said before bursting into tears.

"Good," he said, patting my hand as he handed me his handkerchief. "I know you'll keep your word."

Later that evening, Daddy came back up to my room and handed me a bottle of *Chantilly Lace* cologne he went uptown to buy at Long's Drugstore, just for me. Recently, I ordered two spray bottles of *Chantilly Lace* and wear it often. When I do I think of my dad and the time he taught me about the importance of forgiving others, as well as ourselves.

Chapter 31: He Doesn't Know the Stories

Life has no meaning. Each of us has meaning and we bring it to life.
It is a waste to be asking the question when you are the answer.
—Joseph Campbell

An assortment of household and personal items filled our basement sometime during the late summer of 2010. Andy had spent weeks pulling dishes and photographs, wooden spoons, books, costume jewelry, belts and small objets d'art from Latvia out of boxes and cupboards and carefully arranging them on card tables. Son Peter and daughter-in-law Hsin-Ju were visiting from Connecticut for two-days only. Andy had asked them to come to Grand Rapids to select a few of his parents' belongings to take home with them. Andy had spent weeks after his mother's funeral sorting through hers and his father's belongings. Both his parents were in their early 90's when they died. Neither of them would discuss end-of-life planning or went willingly. His dad, especially, fought to the very end. They were not accustomed to "giving up" or "surrendering" to anything—even death. When death came, as it always does, most of the legal, financial and personal settling of their modest estate, fell to my husband.

As refugees of World War II, Andy's parents, Peter and Mirdza, came to America in 1949 from a displaced persons (DP) camp in Germany where they lived for nearly five years. His parents, his maternal grandmother, Anna Mednis, Andy, 2, and his older brother Ray, 3, had escaped on foot from their home in Riga, Latvia. Younger brother George was born in their German DP camp in 1949. The family landed in Boston with the clothes on their backs, the equivalent of $10 in Dad's pocket, a few hand-carried belongings, and hope in their hearts that they would find freedom, peace and prosperity in America. They knew from living under the threat of the Nazis and the Communists that freedom isn't free. The moment they landed in the U.S., they were ready to roll up their sleeves and work hard without depending on handouts. Sponsored by the Catholic Church in South Haven, Michigan, Mom and Dad ended up as fruit pickers on a farm in South Haven, Michigan, while Omite, his maternal grandmother, took care of the three young brothers.

Andy's dad, also named Peter, had been an attorney for the Latvian government, which is why the Communists wanted to send him to Siberia. Dad's parents owned a large farm in the country southwest of Riga, with horses, orchards, flower and vegetable gardens, and a lovely country home where Andy's parents spent weekends and summers. Andy's mother, a Lutheran by birth, became a Catholic when she married Andy's father in 1940.

Remarkably, none of the belongings Mom and Dad accumulated over their years in Michigan had come with them from Latvia. All those were left behind when the family fled from the Russians after WWII. Some of their Latvian-made belongings came from relatives who traveled back and forth to Latvia after the war. Most of their belongings at the time of their deaths were acquired during their 60 years as American citizens living and working in Michigan.

Andy and I watched in silence as Peter moved from table to table, occasionally picking up an item, turning it over to examine it then putting it down. He had enjoyed a close relationship with his grandparents, having lived with them for two summers when he was a student at the University of Michigan and we were in Saudi Arabia. We assumed he would want something of theirs to pass on to his own two young daughters someday.

"See anything you'd like to take home with you, Peter?" Andy asked as Peter approached the last table.

"Not really, Dad," Peter said, glancing up with a sheepish grin.

My poor husband shrugged his shoulders. "Nothing?" he asked.

Hsin-Ju spoke up giving Andy a sympathetic look. "He doesn't know the stories. None of it means anything to him because he doesn't know what they all meant to Grandma and Grandpa."

Slowly but surely we eventually learn that stories bring meaning to "stuff" so easily tossed away that can be reused and revered for what it meant to those who gave us life. Life is breath, everything else is a story.

Chapter 32: Roots and Wings

The true meaning of life is to plant trees
under whose shade you do not expect to sit.
—Nelson Henderson

Born in Sandusky, Michigan, on April 26, 1906, Sarah Gwendolen Frostic died on April 25, 2001, one day before her 95th birthday. When she was 8 months old, Gwen suffered an unknown illness which left her with a lifelong physical condition similar to cerebral palsy. Growing up, she showed an early interest and aptitude for art. In June 1924, she graduated from Theodore Roosevelt High School in Wyandotte, where she used a band saw to create event posters for her school.

Gwen continued her studies at Eastern Michigan University earning her teacher's certificate and gaining membership in Alpha Sigma Tau sorority. In 1926, she transferred to Western Michigan University and left a year later without completing her degree. She continued her artistic endeavors in metal and plastic, while occasionally teaching. With WWII came a lack of metal to work with and she turned to linoleum block carving. Gwen then turned her linoleum block carving into stationery goods and prints. In the early 1950s she opened up a shop selling these prints, books, and other items in Frankfort, MI. In 1960, she bought 40 acres of land in Benzonia with the intention of moving herself and her shop. On her 58th birthday on April 26, 1964, she opened for business in a building of her own design, and lived there until her death.

I first met Gwen when she spoke to the Petoskey chapter of Zonta, an international service organization of business and professional women. I joined Zonta in 1980, the same year I started my secretarial business. What puzzled me about Gwen's presentation that day was her resistance to new technology. Astute as she was as a business owner, she resisted computerizing her business and even her printing presses. She wasn't one to follow the crowd.

Years later, I stopped to visit with her at her card and gift shop in Benzonia, Michigan. The two of us sat in her office in the back of the shop as she shared with me her philosophy of life. One of the first things she told me was to pattern myself after a tree. She said a tree sends its roots deep into the nurturing earth and spreads its branches up into the sky, making homes for birds, squirrels, ants, and many other living creatures. Storms come and break its branches. Lightening strikes and damages its limbs. Seasons come and seasons go. Through all these changes the tree remains its true self—a tree. Every spring, even the oldest of trees have tiny, little green leaves coming out in the very tips of its branches as it continues to grow and spread its beauty and life-affirming nurturance into the world. Gwen was all about preserving timeless values of the past while embracing future possibilities—as long as the natural world of nature is respected and preserved.

In spite of her physical disabilities, Gwen Frostic's success as an artist enabled her to also be a generous philanthropist. In 2007, the Western Michigan University Board honored her for her $13 million gift, one of the largest single gifts in the school's history, by naming their School of Art the Gwen Frostic School of Art.

After Gwen died, I contacted the owners who purchased her business to see if she had written a memoir. Several days later I received in the mail a complimentary copy of Gwen's lifestory on two pages, written by Gwen herself, in 84 words:

> *She was born ... of that there's no dispute. She goes to bed each night and rises every morning (tho [sic] not so very early), eats breakfast, lunch and dinner ... and sometimes in-between. She always liked to play with blocks. The things boys did seemed best of all. She liked to hammer and to saw. She started school at six. Went through all the grades and college before she tackled business. She wishes there were more to tell ... but that's the story in a shell.*

Gwen was both humble and confident. She lived simply and in tune with the natural world by doing what she loved as poet and artist. While some called her "disabled," Gwen Frostic was a mystic. Awed by nature, she described it poetically in words and in drawings but never explained it scientifically. Guided by her faith in the natural world and sustained by her belief in her own abilities, Gwen has always been and always will be a hero to me.

Chapter 33: Family Stories

We would stand barely a chance in the world if we did not rely from cradle to grave on what has been handed down from those who have lived and worked before us. From agriculture to health care, from education to sanitation, we are the recipients of generations of toil.
—David Whyte

When video news reports from Ukraine showed citizens fleeing their homes and running for their very lives—mothers with children, older and disabled Ukrainians assisted by others—leaving brothers, husbands and sons behind to fight Russians invading their country, I asked myself, could I be as courageous and resilient in similar circumstances? What would I grab going out the door, something I could carry, not knowing when my journey to safety would end, wondering if we'd ever be reunited as a family in a place we could call home?

It didn't take me long to know what I'd take: my copy of *Family Stories* that my two sisters and I compiled into a hardcover book in 2011 as a Christmas gift to our children and grandchildren. This 8.5 by 11-inch book is a collection of stories written about those on both our mother's side, and our father's side, who lived before us, some as far back as the late 1700s, including photographs. All the stories tell of hardships and losses, and how they survived by faith, courage, good fortune, and refusing to give up.

Thanks to our mother and my father's sister who saved decades of memorabilia, letters and newspaper clippings, birth certificates, death certificates and photographs passed on to them, my sisters and I have been able to preserve a distilled version of it all to pass on to our children and grandchildren, and hopefully to more generations to come.

This treasure trove of family history contains lessons learned and passed on by those no longer living, yet their wisdom endures. When I found myself single again at age 37, these family stories from my mother and aunt came to life for me as my comfort and inspiration. Reading about the struggles and hardships my ancestors endured, how they persevered and survived despite personal loss and disappointment, displacement, wars, illness, loneliness, and financial hardships made me realize that if they could survive less than ideal circumstances, I could, too. Reading through them and reflecting on them gave me the strength and will to go on. I saw courage, resilience, decency, strong faith, commitment, forgiveness, sacrifice and integrity, as well as humor, in family members I never met and some I had who were no longer living. I wanted my loved ones coming after me to also be able to someday read these stories, which is why they are so precious to me as I grow older.

This is why I feel it's important for those of us alive today to take the time to write down stories from our own lives about what we've experienced and what we continue to experience as we grow older. Many of us Americans too often forget and take for granted how fortunate we are to live where we live. With all our flaws, we are still the hope of culturally diverse individuals around the world who yearn for freedom and are willing to fight for it in their own countries. I am convinced that the division we are experiencing today in America is temporary and will eventually be the force that causes us to evolve to a higher consciousness enabling us to better cope with the complexity we ourselves have created. As Abraham Lincoln said years ago, "A house divided against itself cannot stand."

Never forget that whatever your situation is today, you are alive because someone before you survived difficult challenges, too, or you wouldn't be here. What stories do you want to leave behind for those coming after you that have taught you lasting life lessons, lessons that inspired you to live a life of purpose and meaning, whether you learned from a parent, grandparent, teacher or coach, even a stranger who said or did something that let you know your life matters?

Chapter 34: Paradox

Genuine Freedom in personal and social relationships
comes from a deep sense of security—knowing who we are,
where we belong, and what is expected of us.
—Sydney Harris

The word "paradox" first caught my attention in 1972, the year my son Bob was born, the same year I bought Sydney J. Harris's *The Authentic Person: Dealing With Dilemma.*

Harris's column in *The Detroit Free Press* was a favorite of mine while living in Petoskey. In a nutshell, he's saying, and I quote, "the dilemmas of modern humanity are mainly caused by the fact that humanity's thinking, feeling and speaking have been conditioned by a 'winners vs. losers' and 'either/or' rather than a 'both/and' mentality."

Although not named as such in the Bible, many spiritual 'teachings', including paradoxes, are found there, especially in the Beatitudes in Matthew's *Sermon on the Mount* where Jesus says those who mourn will be comforted, those who are humble will inherit the whole earth, those who are merciful will be shown mercy and those who are persecuted for doing right will be blessed by God with the Kingdom of Heaven—not the rich, famous and celebrities our culture today holds up as the ultimate of human success.

Harris also says that before the 20th century, while each earlier generation considered themselves "modern," humanity became qualitatively different from our ancestors for the first time in recorded history. Prior to Darwin and his theory of evolution, Einstein and his theory of relativity and Freud's theory of human unconsciousness or 'shadow' causing us to blame others rather than ourselves for the world's faults through scapegoating, we were asleep at the switch, so to speak. We were creating a more complex world without increasing our intelligence, compassion and empathy to make choices and to guide ourselves as members of the human family in a more peaceful, just, and sustainable way.

The most well known example of scapegoating is the crucifixion of Jesus by the Romans who feared his growing numbers of followers, both

Jews and Gentiles. The Roman empire fell in 395 AD yet the teachings of Jesus are embraced by nearly all faith traditions around the globe, which are growing in popularity today despite what we read in the media. Today's seekers are more interested in following Jesus and less interested in religious dogma. Today's youth are increasingly drawn to a deepening spirituality, meaning a more ecumenical understanding and appreciation of the story and purpose of Creation of which we are all a part rather than rejecting one and embracing the other. Knowing this gives me enormous hope for our world.

Another bit of wisdom I've gained, after reading several books by Joseph Chilton Pearce[10], is the difference between intellect and intelligence. Peace said intellect asks, "Can we do it?" Intelligence asks, "Should we do it?" He said it's not an either/or between the two but a both/and. We need to know if we can do it AND if we should do it, as "can we do it" is more about ego and "should we do it" is more about the awareness of what effect it will have on us, others, and our world. Consciousness is knowing that whatever we cause will have an effect.

For those of us who fall prey to fears of gloom and doom and believe American's finest days are behind her, I look to wisdom teachers such as Father Richard Rohr of the Center for Contemplation and Action in Albuquerque, New Mexico.

In his daily e-mail message on January 3, 2021, Father Rohr said, "A few weeks into the pandemic, some people even began using the word 'apocalyptic' to describe what was taking place. Often, this word is used to scare people into some kind of fearful, exclusive, or reactionary behavior, all in expectation of the 'end times'. But the word 'apocalyptic' from the Greek *apokalupsis* really just means 'unveiling'."

Rather than being doomed, we are breaking apart to become more fully conscious as One, in, with, and through diversity, to create a new world for all life, grateful to be alive to learn, laugh and love better.

---

[10] Joseph Chilton Pearce was an American author of a number of books on human development and child development and is best known for his books, The Crack in the Cosmic Egg, Magical Child and The Bond of Power: Meditation and Wholeness. He preferred the name "Joe".

Epilogue

Everyone lives according to some vision, whether it's conscious or not. That vision becomes the hidden force that energizes our motivations. It is important to articulate a vision by which we can live, so we can hold ourselves accountable to those values that are most important, and in so doing, prosper and flourish.
—Pocketful of Miracles by Joan Borysenko

My vision for America is as a united, integrated, both/and country, not as a politically, culturally and racially divided, either/or country we've become since the 1960's. To me, America is more than a country; America is home to those who know freedom is not free and are able and willing to work for it. I see America as a nation of individuals who see diversity as a strength, not a weakness, where all citizens have the freedom to become who they were born to be, to use their innate talents and gifts to create a better life for all citizens.

My view is that if we go back to our roots and core virtues and values our forefathers and foremothers lived by to settle this land from the beginning, we will be reminded that personally and collectively, freedom is hard work. All of us are capable of doing what we can and must in our daily lives to assure that America will always be a welcoming home to those who value freedom, justice and peace. We honor and learn from the past, but we live in the present as we shape our personal and collective future.

When I was a student at Worthington High School from 1957 to 1961, I was a member of the Worthington High School Choir. One of our favorite songs was inspired by *No Man is an Island*, a book written by Englishman John Donne in 1624. Donne is considered the founder of metaphysical poets, and the lyrics were written in 1968 by Joan Baez, American singer, songwriter, musician, and activist.

No man is an island,
No man stands alone,
Each man's joy is joy to me,
Each man's grief is my own.
We need one another,

Life is Breath
Everything Else is a Story

So I will defend,
Each man as my brother,
Each man as my friend.

My second favorite song was inspired by words from *The New Colossus,* a poem by Emma Lazarus, inscribed on the Statue of Liberty. On June 19, 1885, Lady Liberty was delivered to the shores of America as a gift from the French people commemorating their alliance with the United States during the American Revolution. According to Wikipedia, Lady Liberty represents the hope of many French liberals that democracy would prevail and that freedom and justice for all would be attained.

Give me your tired, your poor,
Your huddled masses yearning to breathe free,
The wretched refuse of your teeming shore.
Send these, the homeless, tempest-tossed to me,
I lift my lamp beside the golden door!

My hope is that at least some of what I've shared in my life stories will inspire you to begin writing your own life stories, and that you can and will find support and helpful resources in the appendix that follows.

It seems to me, that herein we see the rare virtue of a strong individual vitality, and the rare virtue of thick walls, and the rare virtue of interior spaciousness. Oh, human! Admire and model thyself after the whale! Do thou, too, remain warm among ice. Do thou, too, live in this world without being of it. Be cool at the equator; keep thy blood fluid at the Pole. Like the great dome of St. Peter's, and like the great whale, retain, O, human, in all seasons a temperature of thine own. — Moby Dick *by Herman Melville*

-o0o-

There is a time in every individual's education when they arrive at the conviction that envy is ignorance; that imitation is suicide; that they must take themselves for better, for worse, as their portion; that though the wide universe is full of good, no kernel of nourishing corn can come to them but through their toil bestowed on that plot of ground which is given to them to till.—Self Reliance by Ralph Waldo Emerson

Flowers unfold slowly and gently, bit by bit in the sunshine
. . . and a soul, too, must never be pushed
or driven . . . but unfolds in its own perfect timing
to reveal its true wonder and beauty.

—The Findhorn Community 1975

APPENDIX

The Pearl of Great Price

*Again, the kingdom of heaven is like unto a merchant man,
seeking goodly pearls: Who, when he had found one pearl
of great price, went and sold all that he had, and bought it.*
— Matthew 13:45-46, King James Version

Even one story or a letter you write and leave behind for your children
and grandchildren, nieces, nephews or friends, that tells them about an
experience you had, a lesson you learned that changed your life for the
better, are like "a pearl of great price." Write about what you want them
to know about you, or your life, something you learned that will help
them live confidently into a future you can only dream about. No
complaining, no negative opinions about the world today, no axes to
grind, no grudges to settle. Rather, share with them what you learned that
made your life, and the world, better. Tell them why, and how, this one
experience gave you hope, strength, confidence in your own ability to
keep going when facing disappointment, loss, or conflicts and
disagreements at home, work and in the neighborhood. Such a story or
letter, in your own words, is an important part of the legacy you leave
behind for future generations to benefit from, a lesson that changed your
life for the better, and hopefully, theirs too.

Guidelines to Consider

1. One size does not fit all. Do this in a way that's comfortable whether
   it's writing a letter in your own handwriting, or writing a story about
   an event in your life when you learned the most valuable lesson
   you've never forgotten, something that guides your way even today.
2. If you have more than one event like the *Pearl of Great Price*, write
   that story, too, and as many stories as you can think of that were life-
   changing experiences and insights still relevant today.

3. Make a list of the 5 or 10 major turning points in your life. Write a story about each one. You don't have to start with the first one. Do them randomly. You can put them in chronological order later.
4. Use writing materials you find most comfortable: (1) computer, or (2) pen and paper, or (3) pencil and paper. If you prefer writing by hand, a spiral notebook with lined, three-ring paper allows you to rip out pages to discard later, or place them into a three-ring notebook as you organize your stories according to a time line or subject matter.
5. Always date each entry.
6. A story has a beginning, a middle and an end. A beginning sets the scene: time, place, characters. A middle describes a turning point, a crisis, an unforeseeable event that brings lasting change. An ending is a resolution of the change that occurred to alter the trajectory of your life. A story can be anywhere from 500 to 5,000 words in length. Advice from E. B. White in his classic, *Elements of Style*: be clear and precise, avoid fancy words, omit needless words.
7. Other story ideas: list values to live by, values you have. List people who inspired you and why. List hobbies you love, and why.
8. Each one of us can choose whether we see our older years as wisdom years, where we reflect on our life with gratitude, humility and humor, or if we are in despair because of regrets, fear of death, fear of the unknown, which Erik Erikson describes in his *Eight Stages of Psychosocial Development* which can be found online.
9. Because I've always believed that the greatest gift we humans have received after the gift of life is the gift of choice, I close with this Bible verse from Deuteronomy 30:19:

> *"I call heaven and earth to record this*
> *day against you, that I have set before*
> *you life and death, blessing and cursing:*
> *therefore choose life, that both thou and*
> *thy seed may live."*

What is Your Most Prized Possession?

One summer in the 1990's, I facilitated a life-story writing workshop in Petoskey, Michigan. I began by giving a brief summary of why I loved life-story writing. I then asked participants to share why they were there.

An attractive, well-dressed, middle-aged woman from Chicago stood up, introduced herself and described a handwritten letter she said was her most prized possession.

"My most prized possession is a handwritten letter from my mother, shortly before she died," she said. "I didn't find it until after she was gone. In it she wrote about how proud she was of my professional accomplishments. She described how she adored me from the moment I was born, and how proud she was of me as a lawyer and volunteer leader in my community. She went on to say how much she loved me and would always be with me in spirit, even after her death."

And then the woman paused. Everyone in the room, including me, thought she was done. But she wasn't.

"While I keep a copy of Mother's letter by my bedside," she said, "the original's in my safety deposit box at my bank. It's my most valuable possession."

As a successful lawyer who never had children of her own, she went on to say she was now writing stories from her own life to leave for her nieces and nephews. She wanted them to know how much she loved and admired them. She also wanted them to know why she made the choices she made, choices that had shaped her life—her career, her volunteer activities, her church affiliation, friendships she made, values she lived by and the causes she supported with her philanthropy.

As it is written in 1 Corinthians 13:13: *And now these three remain: faith, hope and love. But the greatest of these is love.* Memories fade, but the love lasts forever. By writing personal stories about how you learned important life lessons, stories about some of your most enduring and endearing memories, you will enjoy reliving them now yourself and leave them behind to inspire others coming after you.

Quotes for Inspiration

Don't tell people how to live their lives. Just tell them stories and they'll figure out how the stories apply to them. —Randy Pausch, author of *The Last Lecture: Really Achieving Your Childhood Dreams.*

-o0o-

The story of your life is a story only you can write. It's a story without end for your story will live on after you're gone.—Unknown

-o0o-

The world is changed by your example, not by your opinion.
—Paulo Coelho

-o0o-

Anyone who writes down to children is simply wasting his/her time. Write up, not down. —E.B. White, and Gwen Frostic

-o0o-

The two most important days in your life are: (1) the day you are born; (2) the day you figure out why. —Tim Ryan

-o0o-

Of all the pulpits from which the human voice is ever sent forth, none reaches so far as from the grave. —John Ruskin

-o0o-

A miracle is a shift in perception from fear to love—from a belief in what is not real, to faith in that which is. That shift in perception changes everything.—Marianne Williamson

*A hundred years from now it will not matter what my
bank account was, the sort of house I lived in, or the
kind of car I drove... but the world may be different
because I was important in the life of a child.*
—Forest E. Witcraft

-o0o-

*There are two mistakes one can make along the road to truth:
not going all the way, and not starting.*
—Buddha

-o0o-

*The Narrative Paradigm is a theory that suggests
that human beings are natural storytellers and
a good story is more convincing than a good argument.*
—Walter Fisher

-o0o-

*Bear in mind that the wonderful things you learn in your schools
are the work of many generations. All this is put in your hands as
your inheritance in order that you may receive it, honor it, add to it,
and one day faithfully hand it on to your children.*
—Albert Einstein

-o0o-

*Anyone who stops learning is old, whether at twenty or eighty.
Anyone who keeps learning stays young.
The greatest thing in life is to keep your mind young.*
– Henry Ford

-o0o-

I can be somebody's and still be my own.
– *The Missing Piece* by Shel Silverstein

We do not live in the past, but the past in us.
—U.B. Phillips

-oOo-

The path to most hearts is through the brain.
—Peggy Noonan

-oOo-

Do what you love and love what you do.
Work is love made visible.
—Kahlil Gibran

-oOo-

I am a part of all that I have met;
Yet all experience is an arch wherethro'
Gleams that untravell'd world whose margin fades
For ever and forever when I move
—Ulysses by Lord Tennyson

-oOo-

Before you speak, let it pass through three gates:
Is it true? is it necessary? Is it kind?
—Rumi

-oOo-

Never limit your view of life by any past experience.
It is not a question of failing or succeeding. It is simply a question
of sticking to an idea until it becomes a tangible reality.
—Ernest Holmes

-oOo-

If it is to be it is up to me.
—William Johnsen

-o0o-

When we cling to pain we end up punishing ourselves.
—Leo Buscaglia

-o0o-

There was never yet an uninteresting life.
Such a thing is an impossibility.
Inside the dullest exterior there is a drama,
a comedy, and a tragedy.
—Mark Twain

-o0o-

Ultimately, we have just one moral duty:
to reclaim large areas of peace in ourselves.
—Etty Hillesum

-o0o-

Your true vocation is the place where your
deep gladness meets the world's deep need.
— Frederick Buechner

-o0o-

It is something to be able to paint a particular picture,
or to carve a statue, and so to make a few objects beautiful;
but it is far more glorious to carve and paint the very atmosphere
and medium through which we look, which morally we can do.
To affect the quality of the day, that is the highest of the arts.
—Henry David Thoreau

-o0o-

No Day Shall Erase You From the Memory of Time.
—Virgil, in Book IX of "The Aeneid"
This quote is on the wall of the 9/11 museum
in NYC with all the names of those who perished that day.

-o0o-

No one ever made a difference by being like everyone else.
—P.T. Barnum

-o0o-

My religion is kindness.
— The Dalai Lama

-o0o-

The individual of faith, of energy,
of warmth, steps in and does something.
—Vincent Van Gogh

-o0o-

Never forget that justice is what love looks like in public.
—Cornel West

-o0o-

Trifles make perfection, and perfection is no trifle.
—Michelangelo

-o0o-

Find ecstasy in life, the mere sense of living is joy enough.
—Emily Dickinson

-o0o-

Let us temper our criticism with kindness.
None of us comes fully equipped.
—Carl Sagan

-oOo-

Magic is real; Love is greater; Never judge others; Everything is
better with friends; Kindness and goodness always prevail; There's
always far more happening than meets the eye, and nothing is ever lost.
—Mike Dooley

-oOo-

The loudest voices rarely represent the majority. They're usually
speaking for the extremes. You won't understand the views of a group
until you've invited the quieter voices into the discussion. Don't mistake
silence for disengagement. It's often a sign of deep reflection.
—Adam Grant

-oOo-

The first problem for all of us, men and women,
is not to learn, but to unlearn.
— Gloria Steinem

-oOo-

All you have to do is take a close look at yourself
and you will understand everyone else.
—Isaac Asimov

-oOo-

God became human so that humans might become God.
—Saint Athanasius, in *A Beginner's Guide to*
Dante's Divine Comedy by Jason M. Baxter

-oOo-

*Hire people inspired to achieve something big over
people who demand something big before they feel inspired.*
—Simon Sinek

-o0o-

*There is no power on earth that can neutralize the influence
of a high, pure, simple and useful life.*
—Booker T. Washington

-o0o-

Inspiration usually comes during work, rather than before it.
—Madeleine L'Engle

-o0o-

*If I had to say what writing is, we would
define it essentially as an act of courage.*
—Cynthia Ozick

-o0o-

*Writing is the act of saying I, of imposing yourself on other people
of saying listen to me, see it my way, change your mind.*
—Joan Didion

-o0o-

Bibliography

Allen, Marc, *The Greatest Secret of All: Moving Beyond Abundance to a Life of True Fulfillment* ©2008

Arrien, Angeles, *Signs of Life: The Five Universal Shapes and How to Use Them* ©1992

Arrien, Angeles, *The Second Half of Life* ©2007

Atkinson, Robert, *The Gift of Stories: Practical and Spiritual Applications of Autobiography, Life Stories and Personal Mythmaking* ©1995

Baxter, Jason M., *A Beginner's Guide to Dante's Divine Comedy* ©2018

Brooks, Arthur C., *From Strength to Strength: Finding Success, Happiness and Deep Purpose in the Second Half of Life* ©2022

Brumet, Robert, *Birthing a Greater Reality: A Guide for Conscious Evolution* ©2010

Bucko, Adam, *Let Heartbreak Be Your Guide: Lessons in Engaged Contemplation* ©2022

Chittister, Joan, *The Gift of Years: Growing Older Gracefully* ©2008

Clayton, Eric A., *Cannonball Moments: Telling Your Story, Deepening Your Faith* ©2022

Coelho, Paulo, *The Alchemist: 30th Anniversary Edition* ©2018

Contemporary Books, *One Hundred and One Famous Poems* ©1958

Conway, Jill Ker, *The Road from Coorain* ©1989

Delio, Ilia, *Birth of a Dancing Star: My Journey from Cradle Catholic to Cyborg Christian* ©2019

Duffy, Kathleen, *Teilhard's Mysticism: Seeing the Inner Face of Evolution* ©2014

Eger, Edith, *The Choice: Embrace the Possible* ©2017

Eger, Edith, *The Gift: 12 Lessons to Save Your Life* ©2020

Elgin, Duane, *Choosing Earth: Humanity's Great Transition to a Mature Planetary Civilization* ©2020

Fox, Matthew, *A Way to God: Thomas Merton's Creation Spirituality Journey* ©2016

Fox, Matthew, *Naming the Unnameable: 89 Wonderful and Useful Names for God . . . Including the Unnamable God* ©2018

Frank, Anne, *The Diary of a Young Girl* ©1952

Frankl, Viktor E, *Man's Search for Meaning* ©1959

Friedman, Tova and Brabant, Malcolm, *The Daughter of Auschwitz: My Story of Resilience, Survival and Hope* ©2022

Gies, Miep and Gold, Alison Leslie, *Anne Frank Remembered: The Story of the Woman Who helped to Hide the Frank Family* ©1987

Girard, René, *Things Hidden Since the Foundation of the World* © 1987

Harris, Sydney J., *The Authentic Person: Dealing With Dilemma* ©1972

Hollis, James, *Living Between Worlds: Finding Personal Resilience in Changing Times* ©2020

Johnson, Robert A., *Owning Your Shadow: Understanding the Dark Side of the Psyche* ©1991

Lesser, Elizabeth, *The Seeker's Guide: Making Your Life a Spiritual Adventure* ©1999

Levine, Stephen, *Healing Into Life and Death* ©1987

Luke, Helen M., *Old Age: Journey Into Simplicity* ©1987

Lynch, Thomas, *The Undertaking: Life Studies From the Dismal Trade* ©1997

Matousek, Mark, *Writing to Awaken: A Journey of Truth, Transformation & Self-Discovery* ©2017

McKinney, Jane, and McKSchmidt, *Mary, Miracle Within Small Things* ©2023

Meyer, Joyce, *How to Age Without Getting Old: The Steps You Can Take Today to Stay Young for the Rest of Your Life* ©2021

Miller, James E., and Cutshall, Susan C., *The Art of Being a Healing Presence: A Guide for Those in Caring Relationships* ©2001

Montgomery, Ben, *Grandma Gatewood's Walk: The Inspiring Story of the Woman Who Saved the Appalachian Trail* ©2014

O'Donohue, John, *Anam Cara: Spiritual Wisdom From the Celtic World* ©1997

O'Murchu, Diarmuid, *In the Beginning was The Spirit: Science, Religion and Indigenous Spirituality* ©2012

O'Murchu, Diarmuid, *Incarnation: A New Evolutionary Threshold* ©2017

Osbon, Diane K., *A Joseph Campbell Companion: Reflections on the Art of Living* ©1991

Palaver, Wolfgang, *René Girard's Mimetic Theory* ©2013

Pausch, Randy, *The Last Lecture* ©2008

Pearce, Joseph Chilton, *The Death of Religion and the Rebirth of Spirit: A Return to the Intelligence of the Heart* ©2007

Pearce, Joseph Chilton, *The Heart-Mind Matrix: How the Heart Can Teach the Mind New Ways to Think* ©2012

Pennebaker, James W., *Opening Up: The Healing Power of Expressing Emotions* ©1997

Pipher, Mary, *Writing to Change the World* ©2006

Pipher, Mary, *Women Rowing North: Navigating Life's Currents and Flourishing as We Age* ©2019

Rohr, Richard, *Everything Belongs: The Gift of Contemplative Prayer* ©2003

Rohr, Richard, *Falling Upward: A Spirituality for the Two Halves of Life* ©2011

Rohr, Richard, *The Enneagram: A Christian Perspective* ©2013

Rohr, Richard, *Everything is Sacred: 40 Practices and Reflections on the Universal Christ* ©2021

Rolf, Veronica Mary, *An Explorer's Guide to Julian of Norwich* ©2018

Savary, Louis M., *Teilhard de Chardin* The Divine Milieu *Explained: A Spirituality for the 21st Century* ©2007

Shapley, Harlow, *The View From a Distant Star: Man's Future in the Universe* ©*1963*

Singh, Kathleen Dowling, *The Grace in Dying: A Message of Hope, Comfort, and Spiritual Transformation* ©1998

Singh, Kathleen Dowling, *The Grace in Aging: Awaken As You Grow Older* ©2014

Smart, Elizabeth, *My Story* ©2013

Stone, Richard, *The Healing Art of Storytelling: A Sacred Journey of Personal Discovery* ©1996

Strunk, Jr., William, and E.B. White, *The Elements of Style, Fourth Edition, with Revisions, an Introduction, and a Chapter on Writing* ©2000

Taylor, Daniel, *Tell Me A Story: The Life-Shaping Power of Our Stories* ©1996

Teilhard de Chardin, Pierre, *The Phenomenon of Man* ©1959

Teilhard de Chardin, Pierre, *Human Energy* ©1962

Tolle, Eckhart, *The Power of Now: A Guide to Spiritual Enlightenment* ©1999

Van Dyke, Michael, *Radical Integrity: The Story of Dietrich Bonhoeffer* ©2001

Whyte, David, *Crossing the Unknown Sea: Work as a Pilgrimage of Identity* ©2001

Zweig, Connie, *The Inner Work of Age: Shifting from Role to Soul* ©2021

-o0o-

Mark Matousek, award-winning author, teacher, and speaker whose work focuses on transformative writing for personal, professional, and spiritual development. www.markmatousek.com

I also recommend **Deb Moore**, www.thestoriesofyourlife.com, to coach and assist you in writing and publishing your own life story as a timeless treasure for yourself, your family and friends.

Pam's Guidelines for Memoir or Life Story Writing

1. Begin with why, why am I writing this and what do I want to express and share?

2. There is no right, wrong or just one way to write your life story.

3. Honor your ancestors; you're alive because they survived and so can you. Thank those who strengthen you with love and guidance; forgive those for what they did or said that wounded you. Pass on the wisdom you learned without passing on the pain of what they did or said to you. Be your own best friend and let them stay in the past as you go forward in your own life.

4. When you write your life story, don't let anyone else besides you hold the pen.

5. What you can't express you can't heal; write from your head, heart and soul—all three.

6. Reinforce the values you learned, especially those you learned the hard way, for they are like gold.

7. Words have power; choose them carefully. They can and do harm self and others, and they can heal every hurt of the heart.

8. Once in print, always in print; date everything you write when you write it, and read it over carefully before it's printed.

9. We change and evolve, what was written yesterday may not be who we are today, and we'll have more to write tomorrow.

10. We live, love, laugh and learn, and to be able to laugh at ourselves is the best medicine of all.

11. Growing older is inevitable; growing old is optional. Old is stuck in the past. Wise is learning from the past and living in the present to positively affect our future.

12. When telling the truth in an over-arching narrative it's autobiography; if it's fiction, it's fictionalized truth. Stories are stories that stand alone and stand together as life lived, day by day, hour by hour, minute by precious minute.

-o0o-

I know from experience that when two people sit down to tell stories from their lives and to truly listen, something happens. Together they learn, they forgive, they cry, they remember. Something in them moves, even if just a tiny bit. Storytelling and Social Change offers valuable guidance for people who want to use the practice of telling and listening to stories to make a positive difference in their communities.

—Dave Isay, founder and president of StoryCorps[11]

-o0o-

If we could read the secret history of our enemies, we should find in each human's life sorrow and suffering enough to disarm all hostility.

—Henry Wadsworth Longfellow

-o0o-

---

[11] StoryCorps is an American non-profit organization whose mission is to record, preserve, and share the stories of Americans from all backgrounds and beliefs. StoryCorps grew out of Sound Portraits Productions as a project founded in 2003 by radio producer David Isay. Wikipedia

A Story Has . . .[12]

1. A good beginning that gets your attention quickly.

2. At least one character you really care about, a character who stays in your mind.

3. A plot that keeps you interested by setting up a big problem.

4. A big scene where that character takes some action to solve the problem.

5. A good ending that keeps you excited and pulls the whole story together.

---

[12] Taken from the blackboard in the early 1990's in Mr. Waldvogel's 5th and 6th grade English classroom at the Hillsdale Academy, in Hillsdale, MI.

About the Author

Pam's lifelong passion has been and always will be reading books, writing stories and collecting quotes. Throughout her career as a writer of real stories about real people, Pam has learned through firsthand experiences that diversity is a strength, not a weakness. As Pam's sister Barbara always said, "You don't have to make someone else wrong to make yourself right."

Pam's memoir, *Coming Home to Myself,* also available at Schuler Books in Grand Rapids, describes her experiences as a new bride in Riyadh, Saudi Arabia, where she and her husband Andy lived for 18 months after Andy accepted a position as staff rheumatologist at King Fahad National Guard Hospital. Three months after they arrived, Pam applied for and was hired as the first Christian, female, American ex-pat writer for the hospital's Public Affairs Department. After Andy and Pam returned to Grand Rapids, MI, in January of 1991, one week before the Gulf War started, Pam became a free-lance writer in 1992 for Butterworth Hospital and later Helen DeVos Children's Hospital. Now retired, Pam is a member of the Junior Golden Rule Guild of the Butterworth Auxiliary of Corewell Health and Helen DeVos Children's Hospital, and Kappa Alpha Theta Alumnae. Andy and Pam are members of Our Lady of Aglona Parish, the Hauenstein Institute, the Gerald R. Ford Presidential Museum and lifetime members of the American Teilhard Association. They love traveling near and far, including visiting their four married children and their families, all living full and fulfilling lives—some coast-to-coast across the country, some here in Michigan.

www.ingramcontent.com/pod-product-compliance
Lightning Source LLC
Chambersburg PA
CBHW070758120626
46557CB00002B/648